FILES

With thanks to Richard Chapman, the illustrator of this book.

Freud – The Key Ideas

Ruth Snowden

For UK order enquiries: please contact
Bookpoint Ltd, 130 Milton Park, Abingdon, Oxon OX14 4SB.
Telephone: +44 (0) 1235 827720. Fax: +44 (0) 1235 400454.
Lines are open 09.00–17.00, Monday to Saturday, with a 24-hour
message answering service. Details about our titles and how to
order are available at www.teachyourself.com

For USA order enquiries: please contact McGraw-Hill Customer
Services, PO Box 545, Blacklick, OH 43004-0545, USA.
Telephone: 1-800-722-4726. Fax: 1-614-755-5645.

For Canada order enquiries: please contact McGraw-Hill Ryerson
Ltd, 300 Water St, Whitby, Ontario L1N 9B6, Canada.
Telephone: 905 430 5000. Fax: 905 430 5020.

Long renowned as the authoritative source for self-guided
learning – with more than 50 million copies sold worldwide –
the **Teach Yourself** series includes over 500 titles in the fields of
languages, crafts, hobbies, business, computing and education.

British Library Cataloguing in Publication Data:
a catalogue record for this title is available from the British Library.

Library of Congress Catalog Card Number: on file.

First published in UK 2006 by Hodder Education, part of Hachette
UK, 338 Euston Road, London NW1 3BH.

First published in US 2006 by The McGraw-Hill Companies, Inc.

This edition published 2010.

Previously published as *Teach Yourself Freud.*

The **Teach Yourself** name is a registered trade mark of
Hodder Headline.

Typeset by MPS Limited, A Macmillan Company.

Printed in Great Britain for Hodder Education, an Hachette UK
Company, 338 Euston Road, London NW1 3BH, by CPI Group (UK)
Ltd, Croydon, CR0 4YY.

The publisher has used its best endeavours to ensure that the URLs
for external websites referred to in this book are correct and active
at the time of going to press. However, the publisher and the author
have no responsibility for the websites and can make no guarantee
that a site will remain live or that the content will remain relevant,
decent or appropriate.

Hachette UK's policy is to use papers that are natural, renewable
and recyclable products and made from wood grown in sustainable
forests. The logging and manufacturing processes are expected to
conform to the environmental regulations of the country of origin.

Impression number   10 9 8 7 6 5 4
Year   2014 2013 2012 2011

Contents

Meet the author

Welcome to *Freud – The Key Ideas*!

I first became interested in both Freud and his follower Jung (who eventually broke away from Freud) while I was still at school. What really drew me to their work was their shared interest in dreams and the unconscious, and it was this aspect that led me to a decision to study psychology at degree level. As it turned out however, my BSc degree in Psychology at the University of Birmingham was very firmly based on the scientific method and behavioural psychology, and so I was disappointed to find that Freud and Jung's work was not considered worthy of much study. After university I went into teaching for a few years. This proved to be very useful groundwork in preparing me to be a writer, because I had to learn how to explain ideas in ways which most people could grasp easily. My early interest in dreams was somewhat on the back burner at this stage, but I was always interested to listen to children's accounts of their nocturnal journeys.

A necessary career break came while my own three children were small, but it was during this period that I turned once again to my own inner world and began to record my dreams in a dream diary. I also became fascinated by my children's accounts of their own dreams and the way their very individual psyches gradually unfolded. This was the beginning of something big, although I was yet to realize it at the time. Eventually my early interests really came to the fore again and I set up a complementary therapy practice, which offered personal development amongst other things. One of the main approaches I used for this was dream-work and in 1998 I was commissioned to write my first book, *Working With Dreams*. This was published by How To Books, under the name of Ruth Berry. Two years later, in 2000, Hodder published two more books of mine: *Freud: a Beginner's Guide* and *Jung: a Beginner's Guide*. By the time these were followed by the first editions of

Teach Yourself Freud and *Teach Yourself Jung* I had remarried and now write as Ruth Snowden.

I now work full-time as a writer and my main interests lie in the spiritual and the psychological, especially in the interactions between the natural world, human culture and the psyche. Freud and Jung were both deeply fascinated by the same kinds of things and you can read accounts in their work of their studies of ancient history, myth, dreams, synchronicities, the paranormal and world religions. As well as writing for adults, I also write poetry and children's fiction, where I enjoy weaving myths into new stories.

Nowadays, a century after his time, people often make fun of some of Freud's more way-out ideas. But I feel that this is unfair. It is easy to forget that Freud was one of the greatest thinkers of his day and his ground-breaking work has totally changed our way of looking at ourselves and our relationships with others.

Ruth Snowden, 2010

Only got a minute?

▶ Sigmund Freud was a doctor who lived in Vienna. He is famous because he founded a new system of psychology that he called **psychoanalysis**.

▶ Freud began by using **hypnosis** to treat neurotic patients. He decided that neurotic symptoms were caused by repressed sexual experiences.

▶ He explored these suppressed memories using **dream analysis** and his new technique, which he called **free association**.

▶ Dreams are of central importance in psychoanalysis. Freud saw dreams as disguised **wish fulfilments**, mainly harking back to childhood experiences.

▶ Much of Freud's work concerned the **unconscious** mind, which he explored by looking at parapraxes (Freudian slips) and jokes, as well as dreams.

- Freud claimed that the **sexual instinct** was very complex and that it was present from birth. Sexual development could get stuck at any stage.

- His theories about the stages of childhood **sexual development** became a model for social and psychological development generally.

- Freud said that the mind had three different levels: the **id, ego** and **super-ego**. These often worked in conflict with one another.

- Freud said that **civilization** causes conflict within the individual, who has to conform. He saw religion and art as means of escape from the real world.

- Many people have been inspired by Freud and the **psychoanalytic movement** grew to achieve international importance, despite rifts and arguments.

5 **Only got five minutes?**

1 Freud's life and career

Sigmund Freud (1856–1939) is famous because he founded a new system of psychology called **psychoanalysis**. His work largely concerns the unconscious mind and is still the basis of various therapies used today. Psychoanalysis also works with theories about the unconscious, personality development, relationships and society.

2 Freud's early work

Freud's pioneering work helped to cure neurotic symptoms by releasing suppressed traumatic memories. This was called the cathartic method. He suggested that conflict occurred when one part of the mind wanted to release blocked up emotions but another part resisted. This conflict led to a process called resistance. Such ideas gradually led Freud to discoveries about the unconscious.

3 The beginnings of psychoanalysis

Freud claimed that the key to neurosis was the suppressed memory of a childhood sexual seduction. He said that current treatment methods were unhelpful because the patient was not in control. Using his new method, the **free association technique,** he encouraged people to relax and voice whatever thoughts arose. Freud was also beginning to use **dream analysis** to access the unconscious.

4 The Interpretation of dreams

Freud emphasised the importance of dreams because they occur during sleep, when the conscious mind releases its hold. He saw all dreams as **wish fulfilments** and said that dream symbols were often used to disguise childhood sexual issues and prevent them from entering the conscious mind. Exploring the hidden desire symbolised in dreams could therefore help to unravel neuroses.

5 Exploring the unconscious

Freud explored the unconscious by studying **dreams, jokes,** and **parapraxes** (Freudian slips). He decided that there were three states of consciousness:

▶ The **conscious** mind is aware of its thoughts and actions.
▶ The **unconscious** is repressed. Information here cannot easily be accessed.
▶ The **preconscious** is where information is stored but can easily be recalled.

6 Sexual theories

Freud studied what he saw as being **sexual deviations** and drew several conclusions:

▶ The sexual instinct has to struggle against various mental resistances.
▶ It is more complicated than people had previously maintained.
▶ The sexuality of neurotics has usually remained in, or reverted to, an infantile state.

Freud's study of **infantile sexuality** challenged the popular view that sexuality lay dormant until puberty, saying that sexual impulses are present from birth.

7 Going back to childhood

Freud said that personality development depends on a child's progression through biologically determined stages, each concerned with a different source of sexual pleasure.

▶ The **oral stage** focuses on the mother's breast.
▶ The **anal stage** focuses on the anus and defecation.
▶ The **phallic stage** focuses on the genitals.
▶ The **Oedipus complex** develops when the child falls in love with the opposite sex parent.
▶ The **latency stage** – the sexual drive becomes dormant until puberty.
▶ The **genital stage** – the sex drive finally becomes focussed on sexual intercourse with an opposite-sex adult.

8 Seeking an adult identity

Freud proposed a new dynamic model of the mind, involving three main parts: the **id, ego** and **super-ego**. Conflicts between these result in **anxiety** and stress. Unconscious **defence mechanisms** arise in order to protect the ego from too much anxiety. An example is **projection**, when taboo urges or faults are projected outwards onto another person.

9 Freud and society

Freud said that **civilization** is necessary for the survival of the species, but the pressure to conform makes it hard for individuals to be happy. Human nature consists of deep instinctual impulses and therefore we can never totally eradicate evils such as **war**. He maintained that all **art** was the result of the sublimation of libidinous urges; he was also dismissive of **religious teachings**, saying that they were merely created to help people cope with the tensions of civilisation.

10 Psychoanalysis

In 1902 Freud was appointed professor at the University of Vienna. He still faced much opposition, but a small supportive gathering slowly evolved into the **Vienna Psychoanalytic Society**. In 1909 the 'International Journal of Psychoanalysis' was published for the first time. The following year the **International Psychoanalytic Association** was formed. Despite arguments and rifts within the psychoanalytic movement, many influential thinkers have been inspired by Freud and have developed his ideas further.

10 Only got ten minutes?

1 Freud's life and career

Sigmund Freud (1856–1939) was an Austrian doctor who lived and worked in Vienna for most of his life. His work largely concerns the **unconscious** mind. Before Freud, psychologists usually just described and observed behaviour. Freud wanted to go deeper, to analyse and explain it. He said that we have many inner motives for our behaviour, and that these are mostly sexual. Freud is famous because he founded a new system of psychology that he called **psychoanalysis**, which is still the basis of various therapies used today.

Psychoanalysis has three main aspects. Firstly it is a type of **therapy** aimed at treating mental and nervous disorders. Secondly it attempts to explain how the human **personality** develops and how it works. Finally it provides theories about how individuals function within personal relationships and in **society**.

2 Freud's early work

While doing medical research Freud became interested in **hysteria** and **hypnosis**. When he began private practice two main methods of treatment were currently used with neurotic patients: electrotherapy and hypnosis. Freud said electrotherapy was useless: when it *did* seem to work it was only because of the power of suggestion. In other words he was saying that mental processes could affect physical symptoms. This was a very new idea, but Freud was not afraid to go against mainstream thinking. He carried on with his pioneering **cathartic method,** helping to cure neurotic symptoms by releasing suppressed traumatic memories.

Freud's suggested that conflict often arose between two different parts of the mind. One part wanted to release blocked up emotions but another part blocked this by a process of **repression**. Ideas like this gradually led Freud to his discoveries about the unconscious.

---

3 The beginnings of psychoanalysis

At first Freud thought that neurotic symptoms were always caused by traumatic events, but soon he decided that they could be caused by **repressed sexual urges**. Freud attacked current authoritarian methods and developed the **free association technique**, where the patient was encouraged to relax on the couch and feel free to voice whatever thoughts arose.

In 1886 Freud went through a period of depression and carried out extensive self analysis. He became very interested in **dream analysis** as a means of access to the unconscious. He coined the term 'psychoanalysis' in 1896. One of the earliest recorded case histories in psychoanalysis is the analysis of **'Dora'**, which was published in 1905 in a specialist journal.

---

4 The Interpretation of dreams

Dream analysis and free association became the two main therapeutic methods in psychoanalysis. Freud emphasised the central importance of dreams for several reasons:

- ▶ They occur during sleep, when the conscious mind releases its hold and is off guard.
- ▶ He had come to realise that previous methods were too authoritarian.
- ▶ Dream symbols often disguised childhood sexual issues.

Freud saw all dreams as **wish fulfilments**. By exploring the hidden desire symbolized in a dream one could therefore begin to unravel a neurosis.

Freud said that each dream has both a **manifest** and a **latent** content. If the dream is analysed, a hidden wish fulfilment can be found lurking. He suggested that there were various mechanisms such as **symbolization** at work, which allowed the dream wish to be expressed, but in a distorted form.

5 Exploring the unconscious

Freud explored the workings of the unconscious by studying **dreams, jokes,** and **parapraxes** (Freudian slips). He suggested there were three states of consciousness:

▶ The **conscious** mind is the part of the mind that is aware of its thoughts and actions. This is where all conscious thought processes occur.
▶ The **unconscious** is the part of the mind that is repressed. Information here cannot easily be dug out.
▶ The **preconscious** is where information is stored and can easily be recalled when needed.

Freud suggested that two opposing processes controlled normal human behaviour. The **pleasure principle** pushes people towards immediate gratification of wishes. The **reality principle** allows us to delay gratification in order to get on with everyday life. Freud used the word **libido** to describe the sexual drive, which he claimed was the driving force for most behaviour.

6 Sexual theories

Theories about sexuality and **sexual development** were a dominant theme in psychoanalysis. Freud was concerned with ways in which libido can become blocked or re-directed. He extended the concept of what was considered to be 'sexual' in order to support his theory that neuroses were caused by sexual problems.

Freud studied what he saw as being **sexual deviations** and drew several conclusions:

▶ The sexual instinct has to struggle against various mental resistances.
▶ It is a lot more complicated than people had previously maintained.
▶ The sexuality of neurotics has usually remained in, or been brought back to, an infantile state.

The popular view in Freud's day was that sexuality lay dormant until puberty. Freud challenged this view, saying that sexual impulses are present from birth. Childhood and puberty are fraught with sexual pitfalls which can lead to problems and sexual deviations in later life.

7 Going back to childhood

Freud said that personality development depends on a child's progression through biologically determined stages, each concerned with a different source of sexual pleasure:

▶ The **oral stage** (birth to one year). Sexual pleasure is obtained from sucking at the mother's breast.
▶ The **anal stage** (one to three years). The 'potty training' phase, when sexual pleasure is focussed on the anus and defecation.
▶ The **phallic stage** (about three to five years). The genitals become the focus of sexual pleasure and the child starts to masturbate.
▶ The **Oedipus complex** (about four to five years). The sexual focus shifts to falling in love with the opposite sex parent.
▶ The **latency stage**. The Oedipus complex is suppressed and the sexual drive becomes dormant until puberty.

▶ The **genital stage**. The Oedipus complex is finally resolved and the sex drive becomes focussed on sexual intercourse with an opposite-sex adult.

8 Seeking an adult identity

Freud proposed a new dynamic model of the mind, involving three main parts: the **id**, **ego** and **super-ego**. These are not physical parts of the brain but represent different aspects of the way we think. Conflicts between them result in **anxiety** and stress. Anxiety acts as an alarm signal that something is wrong; the commonest cause of anxiety is sexual frustration. A particular source of anxiety is attached to each developmental stage. Unconscious **defence mechanisms** arise in order to protect the ego from too much anxiety. Within reason these are healthy. An example is **projection**, when taboo urges or faults are projected outwards onto another person.

Freud said that **instincts** also affect different aspects of behaviour. **Ego instincts** are self-preserving and concerned with the needs of the individual; **sexual instincts** are concerned with the preservation of the species.

9 Freud and society

Freud said that **civilization** is necessary for the survival and comfort of the species, but it demands great sacrifices from the individual because instinctual urges have to be suppressed in order to conform to the rules. Living in society is therefore difficult and it is hard for people to be happy.

Freud expressed disillusion and bewilderment concerning **war**, saying that deep down human nature consists of instinctual impulses and therefore we can never totally eradicate evil.

He maintained that all art was the result of the sublimation of libidinous urges, likening the artist to a child at play. He was also dismissive of **religious teachings,** saying that they were unscientific and merely created in order to help people cope with the tensions of civilisation.

---

10 Psychoanalysis

In 1902 Freud was appointed as a professor at the University of Vienna. Academics were still reacting with hostility and suspicion to his controversial ideas but gradually a small following evolved into the **Vienna Psychoanalytic Society.** By 1909 Freud was well known internationally and he went to America to lecture. The first **International Journal of Psychoanalysis** was published the same year and the next year the **International Psychoanalytic Association** was formed.

Right from the start there tended to be arguments and rifts within the psychoanalytic movement, mainly because of Freud's emphasis on the sexual. However, many influential thinkers have been inspired by Freud and have developed his ideas further. Methods rooted in psychoanalysis are still used by many therapists. Freud was a prolific writer and his style is easy to follow. His original case histories make particularly interesting reading.

Introduction

Sigmund Freud was a doctor who lived and worked for most of his life in Vienna, Austria. He lived from 1856 to 1939 and he is famous because he founded a new system of psychology that he called 'psychoanalysis'.

> **Psychology** is the scientific study of the mind and behaviour.
> **Psychiatry** is the study and treatment of mental illnesses.
> **Psychoanalysis** is the system of psychology and method of treating mental disorders, originally developed by Freud.
> The words all share the same root in the Greek word **psyche**, which means breath, life or soul.

Before Freud, psychologists usually just described and observed behaviour. Freud wanted to go deeper, to analyse and explain it, and this is why I find his work so fascinating. Gradually, he put together existing ideas with findings from his own studies to create the new system of understanding human behaviour that he called psychoanalysis. He also applied his psychoanalytical theories to his own medical practice in treating mental disorders. Freud's methods were not necessarily successful in healing disturbed people, and most of his theories have since been disproved, but psychoanalysis has survived and evolved and is still the basis of various therapies used today in the treatment of neurosis and psychosis.

> One of the ways in which neurosis and psychosis differ is in their severity. A **neurosis** is a minor nervous or mental disorder. A **psychosis** is a more severe and potentially disabling mental disorder.

The word 'psychoanalysis' covers the whole system of psychology that Freud gradually developed as he worked with neuroses and other mental problems. It has three main aspects:

▶ It is a type of therapy aimed at treating mental and nervous disorders – this is the aspect with which most people are familiar. This therapy is based on dynamic psychology – a system which emphasizes the idea that there are motives and drives behind behaviour. Psychoanalytical therapy works with theories about the unconscious and the ways in which it interacts with the conscious mind. The method was originally based on a free-association process, where the patient is given a word and asked to tell the analyst all the ideas that it brings to mind. This helps the patient to recall repressed experiences that have been pushed out of the conscious mind into the unconscious, and so begin to work through neuroses. (For more about free association, see Chapter 3).

▶ It attempts to explain how the human personality develops and how it works.

▶ It provides theories about how individuals function within personal relationships and in society. These theories attempt to explain human behaviour in a very broad sense, going into areas as diverse as art, literature, religion and humour.

> Dynamic psychology, also known as psychodynamics, studies the ways in which various parts of the psyche relate to mental, emotional or motivational forces, particularly at an unconscious level.

Freud's work largely concerns the unconscious mind and the way its workings relate to neurotic symptoms. The idea is that the unconscious mind contains everything we are not directly aware of in our normal waking life, such as memories, dreams, suppressed feelings and urges, and also biological drives and instincts. Freud decided that the unconscious was the source of much of our behaviour and motivation. He did not invent the idea of unconscious mental processes – in fact, the idea had been around for centuries. As far back as Roman times the writer Juvenal (AD 60–130) wrote, 'from the gods comes the saying "know thyself"', showing that even then the idea was not new. (This saying was written up in the famous temple of the Oracle at Delphi.) But Freud was the first really to apply the idea in his clinical practice and to formulate theories about it, because he lived at a time and place where he was able to bring together many previous ideas. In many ways he was way ahead of his time – his passionate interest in the mysterious world of the unconscious is one that many people share nowadays and that I myself have explored in my work as both therapist and writer.

The **conscious** mind is the part of the mind that is aware of its actions and emotions. The **unconscious** is the aspects of the mind and personality that one is not aware of. These are not physical areas of the brain, of course: they are useful abstract concepts which help us to understand how we think.

Today it is generally accepted that unconscious motives affect our behaviour, and we are all familiar with the idea that our problems are often rooted in childhood trauma and buried emotions. But before Freud it was a different story. One of Freud's own patients, the Wolf Man, a man suffering from a severe neurosis whose case is discussed later in this book, describes the agonizing world he found himself living in before he met Freud. On the one hand, ordinary people focused only on his emotional state and thought he was ridiculously over-reacting to everything. On the other hand, the endless succession of doctors whom he trailed to visit scarcely gave any attention to his emotional state, because for them it was just an unimportant by-product of a physical abnormality in the brain. Meeting Freud, and hearing about his new ideas about the human psyche and the existence of the unconscious, was a revelation to him. Most importantly, he felt validated as a human being rather than simply being labelled as 'sick'. Freud recognized the fact that there is no clear distinction between being 'healthy' and being 'sick', and treated his patients as intelligent people who were struggling to recover.

One of the most interesting aspects of Freud's work – and one to which he gave great emphasis – was his study of dreams and the ways in which they can give us messages from the unconscious. Again, this was by no means a new idea – since as far back as

Biblical times people have been recording their dreams and taking note of their messages. But Freud worked systematically with both his own dreams and those of his patients, gradually building up the beginnings of a language of dreams and the fantasy world of the unconscious. Freud emphasized the idea that buried emotions often surface in disguised forms during dreaming, and that working with recalled dreams can help to unearth these buried feelings. Today, dreams are widely used in many different kinds of psychotherapy. I have been deeply interested in them myself since I was a small child and I have kept a dream diary for many years. My own dreams have always been vivid, colourful and prolific, but in my work as a therapist I have been surprised to discover that not everyone has such a rich and varied dream life.

Freud developed his theories at a time when scientists were beginning to discover how our physical reality is constructed of smaller particles, such as atoms and electrons. Scientific thinking tended to take a very reductionist stance – breaking everything down into its smallest possible parts in order to find out what it is made of and how it works. Similarly, Freud always tried to reduce everything down to what he saw as hard facts, claiming that psychoanalysis always looked at the world in a very scientific way. In actual fact, many of his ideas are impossible to test scientifically; his theories were formed from experiences with a very small sample of middle-class patients and would not stand up to scientific scrutiny today.

However, psychoanalysis soon acquired a huge following – the rigid 'scientific' emphasis appealed to people who wanted to be seen as 'realists'. Like any great leader, Freud's huge self-confidence gave him an air of authority. Before long, a psychoanalytic movement had grown that offered great status to those who belonged to it, and poured scorn on those who challenged it. Indeed, Freud had many critics and his ideas have waxed and waned in popularity ever since. But he undoubtedly changed the way people look at human behaviour, and his influence was so important that there are now hundreds of different forms of psychotherapy.

Freud's work with the unconscious made people begin to look at themselves more honestly and consider what really goes on under the surface. It was Freud who first promoted the idea that giving people plenty of time and really listening to them talking about their problems could help them towards self-understanding. Nowadays this seems really obvious. Although psychoanalysis didn't really prove to be any more or less effective than any of the subsequent methods of psychological therapy, in many cases it enabled people to move on, to some extent, from unhelpful or damaging ways of thinking and behaving. Of course, many of Freud's ideas have proved to be wrong in the hundred or more years that have followed, but they did have a huge influence on modern thought and many of his ideas have been absorbed into everyday life. For example, everyone knows what we mean by a 'Freudian slip', or an 'anally retentive person'.

Freud said that we have many inner motives for our behaviour, and that these are mostly sexual. In fact, he was one of the prime thinkers who helped to make the Victorian prudish attitude to sex a thing of the past. His new theories that sexuality had a part to play in the formation of neuroses caused an enormous uproar at the time, because sex simply was not a topic for open discussion. Nowadays, Freud is often ridiculed for seeming to have claimed that absolutely everything in our minds is sexual. In actual fact, he realized that not everything could be about sex – otherwise neurotic people would not have to struggle to suppress sexual feelings. Freud gradually developed new theories about other motives for our behaviour, such as power or aggression.

Not only did Freud make people look more closely at entrenched beliefs about sex: he also made them more aware of children's emotional needs. In Freud's day, children were 'to be seen and not heard', and were often emotionally neglected. Freud's studies of neurotic patients led him to believe that neurosis often arose as a result of traumatic experiences in childhood. This seems obvious to us now, because children today are seen as real human beings with their own needs and feelings, but Freud was a major pioneer of this school of thought.

As Freud's theories achieved wider acceptance and his ideas began to be absorbed into everyday thinking, they soon began to produce some negative effects too, because the idea of hidden motives caught on. For example, an unselfish person might be seen as secretly indulging in self-punishment, while celibacy might be seen as hiding a fear of sex, or even a nasty perversion of some sort.

Freud had a lively and enquiring mind; he was a skilled physician and scientist; he was also a prolific writer and very good at explaining his ideas in words. All this meant that he acquired many followers and his work has had far-reaching effects. His theories have led to a lot of controversy and debate, and people who pour scorn on his ideas today often make the mistake of taking his ideas out of the context of the period of history in which he lived. Looked at in this light, we can begin to understand that he was a highly gifted and original thinker, and that from his work many new divergent strands of psychology and psychotherapy have developed. This book aims to provide a simple introduction to some of Freud's original ideas, as well as a glimpse into the life of the man himself.

- ▶ Sigmund Freud (1856–1939) was a doctor who lived and worked for most of his life in Vienna, Austria.
- ▶ Before Freud, psychologists usually just described and observed behaviour. Freud wanted to go deeper, to analyse and explain it.
- ▶ Freud founded a new system of psychology called psychoanalysis.
- ▶ Psychoanalysis is the basis for various therapies still used today in the treatment of psychological problems.
- ▶ Psychoanalysis also provides theories about the human personality and how it develops.
- ▶ It also explores human relationships and the functioning of society.
- ▶ Freud was one of the first thinkers to formulate ideas about the unconscious mind and the ways in which it affects our behaviour.
- ▶ Freud's ideas were revolutionary and gave rise to great debate.
- ▶ Freud's thinking has totally altered the way we think today about subjects as diverse as sex, dreams, children's emotional needs, and the hidden motives behind our behaviour.

1

Freud's life and career

In this chapter you will learn:
- *about Freud's personal life and character*
- *key facts about his career*
- *the background to life in Vienna at the turn of the nineteenth century.*

Freud's early life

Sigismund Schlomo Freud was born on 6 May 1856. Later, as a young man, he abbreviated his name to Sigmund Freud. He was born in Freiberg, Moravia, which was then part of the Austro-Hungarian Empire. The town is now Pribor in the Czech Republic. In 1860 his father ran into business problems and the family moved to Vienna, Austria, where Freud lived for most of his life. When Freud was born he was still partly enclosed in a foetal membrane (commonly called a 'caul'), an occurrence which, in folklore, is held to be an unusual and lucky portent. His mother took this to be a sure sign of future fame.

When Sigmund was born, his father Jakob Freud was 40 and already had two children, Emmanuel and Philip, from a previous marriage. Jakob was 20 years older than his wife Amalie, who was Sigmund's mother. Even Emmanuel was older than Amalie and already had children of his own by the time Sigmund was born – so

Sigmund was born an uncle, a year younger than his nephew John who was one of his first playmates.

Freud was the first of Amalie's eight children and he was her firm favourite, 'my golden Sigi'. He later said that this gave him a feeling of invincibility and a great will to succeed. He also attributed his success to the fact that he was Jewish. Although the family was Jewish by descent, they did not practise the Jewish religion. Being Jewish was difficult because there was a lot of anti-Semitism at the time in Vienna, where most people were Roman Catholics. Two of young Sigi's boyhood heroes were Oliver Cromwell, who was definitely anti-establishment, and Hannibal, the Carthaginian leader who got the better of the Romans. Later, when he encountered anti-Semitism at university, it seems to have spurred Freud on still further to prove himself as an independent thinker. Although he never followed the Jewish religion and referred to himself as 'a Godless Jew', Freud was always very proud of his cultural heritage and had many Jewish friends.

Young Sigi was an enthusiastic student at school and his family was very ambitious for him. He soon mastered Greek, Latin, German, Hebrew, French and English, and by the age of eight he was reading Shakespeare. As if all this wasn't enough, he also taught himself the rudiments of Spanish and Italian! He went into secondary school a year early and his education there emphasized classical literature and **philosophy**, which greatly influenced his later thinking and writing. His favourite authors were two of the greatest literary figures of Western Europe – writer and philosopher Goethe, and poet and playwright Shakespeare.

Insight

Philosophy investigates the underlying nature and truth of knowledge and existence. It has a critical, systematic approach, involving a great deal of reasoned argument. This is the way of thinking that Freud always tried to adhere to (with mixed success – for example, read about the Oedipus Complex in Chapter 7).

Needless to say, Sigi often came top of his class – in fact he did it six years running, which must have annoyed his classmates considerably! He was obviously pushed to succeed by his family and teachers, and the lives of the whole family revolved around his all-important studies. He had his own room in the crowded home, while all the rest of his siblings had to share. He even ate his evening meal apart from the others, and when his sister Anna's piano playing distracted him from his studies, his parents had the instrument removed from the apartment.

Jakob Freud was a wool merchant, but he was not very successful financially. He was married three times and had a lot of children, so he was not able to support Sigmund financially later on.

Freud's family background and psychological make-up are obviously important because they influenced his later thinking and gave rise to some of his theories about childhood development.

Sigi had his own room in the crowded house.

Vienna and the society in which Freud lived

Freud had rather a love–hate relationship with Vienna. This was probably because the place fostered all sorts of new ideas, but simultaneously disapproved of them in many ways. Freud was often critical of Viennese people and yet he was very reluctant to leave the city. Several aspects of Viennese society were important in influencing Freud:

▶ *It was a very* **bourgeois** *society – middle class, materialistic and conservative in its attitudes.*

Insight

The word bourgeois is often used in a derogatory way to refer to the capitalist, non-communist way of thinking, which is assumed to be self-seeking, materialistic, dull and unimaginative.

▶ *It was in a state of economic decline. This led to unemployment, poverty and overcrowding.*
▶ *People had a very prudish attitude towards sex, which meant that 'nicely brought-up' girls were appalled when they finally found out what sex involved. At the same time, there was a moral decline that led to a lot of prostitution. This is the kind of dual standard that might have led Freud to consider the significance of the* **unconscious**.
▶ *Men were still thought of as being vastly superior to women. Freud didn't seem to realize, in his own self-analysis, that there was anything wrong with this attitude. (This shows just how inexact a science* **psychoanalysis** *can be!)*
▶ *The prevailing culture was strongly anti-Semitic. This made it hard for the struggling young Freud to advance his career.*
▶ *New ideas of social reform were creeping in, such as early feminist ideas and Social Democracy (a form of Marxism).*
▶ *Scientific views were changing, and the ferment in politics, philosophy, social structure and science was also being reflected in the arts.*

All in all, Vienna towards the end of the nineteenth century was a hothouse of social change and new ideas – a very stimulating place to be living. Its location at the crossroads between East and West meant that it was a very cosmopolitan place – its citizens included Germans, Jews, Poles, Hungarians, Italians and Czechs, to name but a few, and a dozen different languages were widely spoken, including the local dialect. Until 1806 Vienna was the capital of the Holy Roman Empire, and subsequently the seat of the Habsburg dynasty up until 1918.

The Viennese people loved social occasions, and frequently went to large elaborate balls and other social gatherings, such as picnics in the woods in the surrounding hills. Royalty and gentry paraded about in gilded carriages; there were bands in the People's Garden, and a huge funfair at the Prater (a park), with a giant Ferris wheel added in 1873. Coffee houses were everywhere, and people met in them to discuss social affairs, music, literature and the theatre. Great names such as Mahler and Bruckner were being added to the long tradition of musicians who had worked in Vienna, including Mozart and Beethoven. Art flourished too, and the city was a centre for fine porcelain, embroidery, gilt work and architecture.

Because of this intellectual, cosmopolitan environment and his excellent education, Freud was influenced by thinkers from a very wide field and drew on ideas and medical knowledge from throughout Europe. Vienna probably had the finest doctors and hospitals in Europe – there was a saying at the time: 'If you must fall ill, then do so in Vienna.' It was certainly a stimulating environment for a young man just beginning his medical career.

A brief outline of Freud's career

Freud's early ambition had been to study law, but when he entered the University of Vienna in 1873 it was to study medicine.

While at medical college, he specialized in **neurology** and **histology**.

> ## Insight
> The word neurology (or more correctly, neuropathology) is used to refer to the medical discipline that deals with disorders of the nervous system. Histology studies the microscopic anatomy of cells and tissues in both plants and animals.

Freud finally graduated as a Doctor of Medicine in 1881. He would have liked to stay in research, but growing financial pressures and the fact that by now he wanted to get married and support a wife and family, meant that he had to practise as a doctor. He spent the next three years gaining medical experience at the Vienna General Hospital, preparing to enter medical practice.

In 1885–6 Freud spent a few months in Paris, studying with a famous neurologist called Charcot. Charcot was experimenting with **hypnosis** to help cases of **hysteria**, which is a nervous disorder with varying symptoms. This experience was very important because it led Freud to the idea that the mind, as well as **organic disease**, could affect physical symptoms. He gradually developed this theory with the help of a friend and colleague called Josef Breuer.

> ## Insight
> Hypnosis is a state similar to sleep or deep relaxation, where the patient is still able to respond to the therapist and is open to suggestion.
>
> In modern common speech hysteria describes a state of unmanageable fear or emotional excess. In Freud's day it referred to a medical condition where strong emotions often became centred on a specific body part, causing psychosomatic symptoms. Only women were thought to suffer from this (see Chapter 2). The word is not usually used in modern psychiatry.

In 1886 Freud entered private medical practice in Vienna and began his own work on hysterics. From this work he developed the ideas that were gradually to evolve into psychoanalysis. In 1891 he moved to a flat in Berggasse 19, which was made into the Freud Museum Vienna 80 years later.

Right from the start of his career, Freud encountered violent opposition from many other members of the medical establishment, because his ideas were so unusual and disturbed the status quo. Undeterred by this, Freud continued his interest in **neuropathology** and his first published book, *On Aphasia*, appeared in 1891. **Aphasia** is a neurological disorder where the patient is either unable to recognize words, or unable to pronounce them.

Insight

Aphasia is often caused by damage to areas of the brain that are concerned with language.

This was to be the first of many publications throughout Freud's life. It soon became clear to him that psychological disturbances were indeed at work in many cases of mental illness, as he had begun to think while working with Charcot in Paris. This idea was to be the basis of his life's work and one of the main ways in which it differed from that of his contemporaries.

Insight

An organic disease relates to particular body structures or functions. Nowadays we are also very familiar with the idea of psychosomatic diseases, which are thought to be caused by an interaction of mind and body. This idea was very new in Freud's day.

Another book, *Studies On Hysteria*, written jointly with Josef Breuer, appeared in 1895. In the same year, Freud for the first time analysed and wrote about one of his own dreams, subsequently known as 'The Dream of Irma's Injection'.

At first Freud's work concentrated on looking at the causes and treatment of **neurosis**. Gradually, he expanded his theories and became interested in the way the human **psyche** develops. For the next five years, from 1895 to 1900, he developed many of the ideas that are the basis of psychoanalytical theory and practice. He coined the word 'psychoanalysis' in 1896.

In 1897, when Freud was 41, his father died. Following this he entered a period of psychological turmoil that might nowadays be seen as a mid-life crisis. But rather than sinking into depression and lethargy, Freud set to work on his own psychoanalysis. This involved a lot of introspective work, examining his own dreams and fantasies, and led to the publication of his book *The Interpretation of Dreams*, which he considered to be his most important work. Published in 1899, it shows a printing date of 1900 in order to coincide with the new century and give it a feeling of being at the cutting edge.

His first analysis of a patient was of a young girl called Dora during the following year, 1901. This was also the year of publication of his next book, *The Psychopathology of Everyday Life*. At first his ideas had been received with much hostility, but in 1902 he was appointed professor at the University of Vienna and he founded a psychological society called the Wednesday Society, which met weekly at his own home. This gradually evolved, and by 1906 this group of admirers had grown to include some very famous names such as Otto Rank, Carl Jung, Eugen Bleuler, William Stekel and Alfred Adler. The group expanded further and became the Viennese Association of Psychoanalysis in 1908, thus starting the psychoanalytical movement.

The same year saw the first Congress of Freudian **Psychology** in Salzburg, which was attended by about 40 representatives from five countries. The next year, 1909, Freud achieved transatlantic fame when he was invited to lecture at Clark University in Worcester, Massachusetts in the USA. From then on, the psychoanalytical movement attained worldwide recognition, and an organization called the International Psychoanalytical Association was founded during the same year. A well-known periodical, The *International Journal of Psychoanalysis*, was later founded in 1920.

Freud was a prolific writer and carried on writing throughout his long life, constantly exploring new ideas and revising his old theories. His work is very readable and he expresses his ideas clearly. The first volumes of his collected works appeared in 1925 and they finally extended to 24 volumes. However, most of his theories are explained in two books: *Introductory Lectures on Psychoanalysis* and *New Introductory Lectures on Psychoanalysis*. The first of these is a review of Freud's theories and the position of psychoanalysis at the time of the First World War. It is based on a series of lectures that Freud gave in 1916 and 1917. Later, he gradually added to and revised some of the ideas from these lectures and near the end of his life, in 1932, the second book was published. This further set of lectures was never actually delivered – it was intended more as a supplement to the first set.

In 1930 Freud was honoured with the Goethe Prize for Literature, and in 1935 he was elected an Honorary Member of the British Royal Society of Medicine.

Freud's work falls into four main phases:

▶ 1886–96
   Studies on the causes and treatment of neurosis, working with neurotic patients. At first he concentrated on using hypnosis, but later he developed other forms of therapy, based on the free-association method, which gradually evolved into psychoanalysis. During this period he published his first books: On Aphasia; Studies On Hysteria.
▶ 1897–1900
   Freud worked very much alone, doing a lot of self-analysis and developing ideas about the sexual origins of neurosis. This was the period during which he developed many of his ideas about psychoanalysis. At the end of this period he produced two very important books: The Interpretation of Dreams; Psychopathology of Everyday Life.
▶ 1900–14
   Freud began to formulate new theories about the origins of neurosis, which led to a whole system of ideas about how the psyche develops from birth onwards. The psychology that he

*developed at this stage is often called id psychology. The id is
the oldest part of the mind, from which all other structures
develop. It is unconscious and it is concerned with inherited,
instinctive impulses. During this period of his life, Freud wrote
several more important books: Three Essays on the Theory of
Sexuality; Jokes and Their Relation to the Unconscious; Totem
and Taboo.*

▶ 1914 onwards
*The First World War made Freud look at people's behaviour
in new ways, as he realized that aggression, as well as sexual
urges, could be an important factor in behaviour. He began
to develop theories about the whole personality and the
ways in which people relate to others. This is known as ego
psychology. The ego is the part of the psyche that reacts to
external reality. It is the part of the psyche which a person
thinks of as being the 'self'. Freud wrote many more books
during this period of his life. (For a full list, see Taking it
further at the end of the book.)*

Freud's private life and personality

FAMILY

In 1886 Freud at last married his fiancée, Martha Bernays. Their
first child, Mathilde, was born the following year. Eventually they
had five more children: Jean-Martin (1889), Olivier (1891), Ernst
(1892), Sophie (1893) and finally Anna (1895), who later became a
psychoanalyst. The family often struggled financially, and in 1918
Freud lost a lot of money that had been bound up in Austrian State
bonds. Martha was utterly devoted to Sigmund's happiness and
well-being, and she insisted that in the 53 years of their marriage
not one angry word was spoken between them. Some may question
the truth of this! Whatever else is true, it seems that the couple
gave up sex fairly early on, although this may have been partly
for fear of producing yet more children – birth control was still
very unreliable. However, it does seem that Freud's home life was
probably pretty tranquil and harmonious and that he was firmly

established as the head of the family, which no doubt gave him a stable and secure basis for working in peace.

FREUD'S CHARACTER

In academic circles Freud was often seen as opinionated and rather peculiar, so that much of his work was done in what he called 'splendid isolation', just as it had been from boyhood. He obviously had outstanding intellect, but by his own admission he had a rather neurotic, obsessive personality and could not imagine a life without work. He wrote incessantly and much of his writing was done on his days off, or even after a busy day seeing his patients.

Freud's obsessive personality meant that he was the kind of person who has to do everything meticulously and accurately and he liked to be in control. This can be seen in various ways outside of his work. He was very superstitious about certain numbers – for instance, he became utterly convinced that he would die at 61 or 62, because of a series of rather tenuous coincidences to do with odd things like hotel room numbers. This kind of thinking is the downside of the type of self-controlled personality that is obsessional enough to produce the astonishing volume of work that Freud did. In extreme cases it can lead to what is known as an obsessional neurosis, where the sufferer is driven by endless compulsive rituals, and becomes unable to function normally.

Freud was a great collector of antiques, fired by his earlier classical studies and his interest in ancient history. He accumulated vast numbers of antique statuettes and other artefacts that are still on display in his study at 20 Maresfield Gardens, Hampstead, in London, which is now part of a Freud Museum. They are crammed in all over the place, showing that he was not particularly interested in their artistic value, but more in the feeling of connection with the past that they gave him and the sheer pleasure of collecting them.

His compulsive streak shows up again in the fact that he smoked cigars heavily nearly all his life and found it impossible to stop, even when he was diagnosed with oral cancer in 1923 and realized

that the tobacco was doing him no good. It was not until he had a
heart attack in 1930 that he finally gave up.

FRIENDSHIPS

Freud's friendships tended to be fairly intense, although he was
also prone to falling out with people. This was characteristic of
the way in which he related to friends – he would grow to admire
someone greatly and value their moral support, but at the same
time competitive aspects would gradually creep in and finally
destroy the relationship.

This happened in Freud's relationship with Josef Breuer, who was a
highly respected and successful physician in Vienna. He befriended
Freud and even lent him money. Their relationship became so close
that Freud named his first child Mathilde after Breuer's wife. For
some time Freud was quite dependent on Breuer, but eventually
a rift occurred when Breuer simply could not agree with Freud's
insistence upon sexual motives for everything. By the time their
joint publication *Studies On Hysteria* was published in 1893 their
friendship had already ended. Years later, after Breuer's death,
Freud was greatly moved to find out that his friend had continued
to follow his career with great interest even after the rift between
them had occurred.

Some of Freud's friends had theories that were considered even
more bizarre than Freud's. Breuer suggested that Freud should meet
Wilhelm Fliess, a nose and throat physician from Berlin, when Fliess
was in Vienna for a medical conference in 1887. A strong bond
gradually developed between the two of them. Fliess was obsessed
with the numbers 23 and 28, and developed his own scientific theory,
called 'vital periodicity', involving these numbers. He decided that all
vital processes went in cycles of 28 days for women and 23 days for
men, and went on to suggest that all sorts of useful predictions could
be made from this, such as how long it would take to recover from
an illness and even the likely date of a person's death.

We now know that this idea is not quite as mad as it seemed – it
was the forerunner of the idea of biorhythms. Some of Fliess's

other ideas were madder. For example, he thought the nose was an important sexual organ and that the state of the nose reflected various sexual disturbances. This theory has yet to be proved! However, Freud's friendship with Fliess was typical in that the two men exchanged many ideas and Fliess acted as a useful critic and advisor to Freud until their inevitable falling-out in 1900–01. Fliess was the first person to suggest to Freud the idea of researching jokes and popular fantasies in the light of psychoanalysis. Letters from Freud to Fliess, collected together by Marie Bonaparte in 1938, show the development of his psychoanalytical thinking. Unfortunately, Fliess's replies were either lost or destroyed by Freud.

Fliess thought the nose was an important sexual organ.

BELIEFS AND OTHER INTERESTS

Early on Freud may have dabbled in the Kabbala, the esoteric branch of Jewish mysticism. He belonged to a Jewish society called B'nai B'rith and enjoyed weekly games of taroc, a complicated and popular card game which some people think is based on the

Kabbala. The taroc deck varies in size, but it includes 22 trump cards from the tarot, which are rich in symbolic imagery. The symbolism on these cards may well have set Freud on the path towards his first ideas about the unconscious: it was at this time that he presented his first ideas about dream interpretation. This information has been largely suppressed, probably because it wasn't approved of in Freud's contemporary society, with its rising tide of fierce anti-semitism. Later Freud strongly disapproved in public of what he called 'the occult' (see Chapter 10).

When he did take some time out from work, Freud enjoyed going for long walks with his family and looking for mushrooms. People often think of him as a stern patriarch, but in fact his children recalled plenty of happy days when he stopped working and took them for family outings. He never bought a lot of clothes: in fact, he is reported to have only ever had three suits, three sets of underwear and three pairs of shoes at a time. However, he was not mean and later in life gave financial support to various friends, patients and students. He enjoyed literature, but unlike many in Vienna he was not particularly keen on music, apart from opera.

Following his diagnosis with cancer, Freud suffered many painful medical treatments and surgical operations. However, he continued to write for the remaining 16 years of his life after the diagnosis of cancer – mainly philosophical and cultural publications. His autobiography reveals very little detail of his personal and private family life, and he deliberately destroyed a lot of letters and personal documents, first in 1885 and then again in 1907. Even though he was fascinated all his life by trying to probe other people's minds, he was obviously keen to keep his own affairs private. This might reflect a certain amount of insecurity: it is certainly true that right from the early days of the psychoanalytic movement he was very intolerant of people who disagreed with his fundamental tenets, and took their subsequent defections as personal betrayals.

All this may make it seem as if Freud was a remote and inaccessible figure, but this was not the case. An interesting first-hand account of meeting Freud is given by the Wolf Man. He describes his appearance as being 'such as to win my confidence immediately'. Freud was of medium height and build, correctly dressed, with a long face and a neat beard. His dark, intelligent eyes regarded the Wolf Man penetratingly, but without causing him the slightest feeling of discomfort. He came across as being very self-assured and calm, and the Wolf Man remarks that he had the feeling of encountering a great personality.

The Wolf Man goes on to say that Freud's consulting rooms were not at all clinical. In fact, they struck him as being more like an archaeologist's study than a doctor's office. Fascinating ancient artefacts were everywhere and on the walls were stone plaques depicting scenes from ancient history. Freud explained to him that his love of archaeology was akin to his work as a psychoanalyst, in that he must uncover layer after layer of the patient's psyche until reaching the deepest and most valuable treasure.

Potted plants and warm curtains and carpets made the place feel cosy, and the windows opened onto a little courtyard. The Wolf Man always felt a sense of sacred peace and quiet there. For him, the place was a sanctuary from the hustle and haste of modern life – a place where, for a brief time, one was sheltered from one's day-to-day troubles.

So, Freud was a deeply private person, but by no means unapproachable. And he had his reasons for keeping himself fairly aloof, these being to protect his professional reputation and his family.

In 1938 the Germans occupied Austria, and Vienna became a very dangerous place for anybody Jewish. Freud and his family fled to England, where he was spared the horrors of the Holocaust because he died in London on 23 September 1939. He was the grandfather of painter Lucian Freud and comedian and writer Clement Freud, and the great-grandfather of journalist Emma Freud and fashion designer Bella Freud.

THINGS TO REMEMBER

▶ *Freud is famous because he founded a new system of psychology that he called psychoanalysis.*

▶ *He lived and worked for most of his life in Vienna.*

▶ *Freud was married and had six children.*

▶ *He became interested in hypnosis while studying in Paris.*

▶ *Freud's work largely concerns the unconscious.*

▶ *He said that we have many inner motives for our behaviour, and that these are mostly sexual.*

▶ *Freud's work falls into four main phases:*

▶ *Studies on the causes and treatment of neurosis.*

▶ *Developing ideas about the sexual origins of neurosis.*

▶ *Ideas about how the psyche develops from birth onwards – often called id psychology.*

▶ *Theories about the whole personality and the ways in which people relate to others. This is known as ego psychology.*

2

Freud's early work

In this chapter you will learn:
* *about Freud's medical training and early scientific research*
* *the background of nineteenth-century scientific and moral thinking*
* *Freud's first ideas about the unconscious.*

Freud's medical training

Freud entered the University of Vienna in 1873 to study medicine.
Right at the beginning of his training he became very interested
in zoological research. From 1876 to 1882 he carried out research
at the Physiological Institute, under the guidance of Ernst Wilhelm
von Brücke, one of the most eminent scientific scholars of the day.
Freud greatly admired Brücke, who was a man of great intellect.
He described him as being the greatest authority he had ever met,
and he was hugely influenced by his way of thinking. Brücke
demanded extremely high standards of his students – meticulous
observation and recording – and many of them were in awe of
him. Freud looked up to him as a sort of father figure, and tried
to emulate him as much as possible.

Brücke was dedicated to the mechanistic approach to scientific
research, which held that all biological processes could be

explained in terms of physics and chemistry. This approach was still unpopular early in Freud's life, because it ruled out **vitalist** thinking in science.

> ## Insight
> The mechanistic view sees a person as a machine, whose life processes and behaviour are determined by physical and chemical causes. Vitalism takes the opposite viewpoint, saying that life processes cannot be explained by the laws of physics and chemistry alone. Heavily influenced by religious dogma, it assumes that non-material forces are at work in biological processes.

Freud rejected vitalist ideas and, following Brücke's teaching, he became convinced that all biological processes follow a rigid pattern of cause and effect. This way of thinking – the **determinist** stance – assumes that even the workings of a person's mind can be explained by strict physical laws.

> ## Insight
> Determinism is a popular philosophical stance. It proposes that every event, including what goes on in the human mind, is caused by a prior event or a series of prior events.

During his clinical training, Freud was influenced by one of his tutors, Theodor Meynert, to specialize in neurology. He was particularly interested in neuropathology – the study of diseases of the nervous system. He did not finish his medical training until 1881, so the course took him three years longer than was normal. This was because he really enjoyed research and his interest lay more in this direction than in actually becoming a doctor. The scientific method involved systematically observing, measuring and experimenting. This kind of work would also have been fundamental to Freud's other specialism, histology, which is about the study of cells and tissues. This would have involved a lot of painstaking, meticulous work using a microscope, which would have suited Freud's orderly, methodical way of thinking very well.

Scientific research

During his research work, Freud was given an assignment to investigate the sex organs of eels, about which nothing was known at the time. He also studied the nervous system of lampreys (a kind of fish), and his first published article was on this subject. He wrote 20 or so neurology papers between 1887 and 1897.

The **mechanistic** scientific view insisted that the mind of a human being and that of an animal such as a frog differed only in their complexity. Even ideas were held to be merely the result of a complicated neurological process. This deterministic view was to remain with Freud throughout his life. He believed that all psychological phenomena, even fantasies and feelings, rigidly followed the same principle of cause and effect.

Freud spent some time studying the effects of cocaine, even injecting it into himself when he discovered that it helped him with bouts of depression and low energy. The drug was not prohibited at the time because its harmful effects had not yet been discovered – in fact, it was sometimes prescribed as an anti-depressant. Freud became interested in research into using cocaine as an anaesthetic, hoping that this might pave the way to fame and fortune. When other researchers did, in fact, prove the drug to be useful in this way the market for it expanded enormously in 1884. In 1885 it was used on Freud's father to perform a successful eye operation. Freud even sent some to his fiancée Martha, 'to make her strong'. However, people soon began to become addicted to the drug and its negative effects became clear. Freud realized after this that one had to be very careful when doing scientific research. He continued to use the drug himself occasionally, but fortunately he never became addicted to it.

Freud would have happily stayed in medical research, but he realized that he would not have enough money to support a wife and family. He decided that he would have to go into medical practice and spent the next three years gaining practical medical experience at Vienna General Hospital. In 1885 he was appointed as a lecturer in neuropathology at Vienna University. In the same year, he wrote an essay called *Project for a Scientific Psychology*. This shows that he was already beginning to embark on a lifelong quest to bridge the gap between the exact science of neurology and the newly evolving science of psychology, which was still heavily influenced by philosophical thinking.

Hysteria and hypnosis

In 1885 Freud won a scholarship to study in Paris under the eminent neurologist Jean-Martin Charcot. The few brief months that Freud spent working with him during 1885–6 were to have a profound effect upon his thinking. Charcot was one of the great celebrities of the day, known as the 'Napoleon of Neuroses'. He was frequently asked to attend rich and aristocratic sick people all over the world. He was a man of enormous charisma, and Freud was to fall under his spell, looking up to him to such an extent that he named his first son after him. Charcot was working with cases of paralysis, trying to discover a way of establishing whether they were the result of organic disease in the nervous system – i.e. disease relating to particular body structures or functions – or whether they were hysterical – that is, neurotic in origin. He hoped to develop a diagnostic technique that would distinguish between the two types of paralysis.

Doctors found hysteria interesting for several reasons:

▶ *The symptoms were very varied. They included memory loss, hallucinations, loss of speech, sleepwalking, paralysis, fits, fainting, loss of sensation or numbness in various parts of the body, and even curious symptoms such as arching over backwards in bed in a rigid bow shape. These symptoms were also highly unpredictable – sometimes they would disappear completely for no apparent reason, only to reappear in full force later.*
▶ *Only women were thought to suffer from hysteria. In fact, the word hysteria is derived from a Greek word hustera, meaning*

> *'womb'. Charcot disagreed with this and said that men could have hysteria too.*
> ▶ *Hysteria baffled doctors because it didn't fit in with the anatomy of the nervous system. For example, an arm might be paralysed exactly up to the shoulder, but the nerves don't actually stop there.*

Nobody knew what caused hysteria and there was no cure. Often, patients were accused of faking it and their fate was a sad one – they were frequently locked away in mental hospitals. Charcot discovered that under hypnosis the symptoms could sometimes be made to vanish at the doctor's suggestion, but they would then often reappear as the person emerged from the trance state.

This led Charcot to understand that a patient's own ideas could affect the area of a paralysis. He realized that a person's paralysis sometimes stopped at a neat line because the person *thought* that the limb began or ended at that line, whereas these neat lines did not correspond with the actual physiology of the nervous system. Charcot soon discovered that this type of paralysis could be cured, or even induced, by post-hypnotic suggestion. For example, he could give someone under hypnosis the suggestion that their arm would become paralysed when they woke up.

People who had received post-hypnotic suggestions like this were indistinguishable from others who were actually suffering from hysteria. Although they could not recall the suggestions made to them under hypnosis, they would show similar symptoms of pain, loss of memory, shaking, trembling or paralysis. Charcot was interested in experimenting with this, and gave fascinating demonstrations in front of impressed audiences. Freud took the whole idea a stage further, hoping that if he could unravel the mystery, these discoveries might bring him the fame and fortune he had failed to gain from his research into cocaine.

This was a risky area to get into because at that time hypnosis was better known as a fairground attraction, often preying upon gullible and credulous audiences. However, Freud was undeterred and began to ask questions that Charcot had not thought of.

By looking at things in a fresh light he developed two new ideas that were to become very important in the therapeutic field:

▶ *To understand hysteria one needed to look at the patient's psychology, rather than just neurology.*
▶ *The unconscious mental processes that produce hysterical symptoms actually go on in the minds of all people at levels of which they are not fully aware. These processes can affect people's behaviour. Freud realized that although a patient's behaviour could be affected by hypnosis, they often did not recall what had happened during the session. This was the beginning of Freud's development of psychoanalysis.*

Freud's new ideas may seem rather unstartling to us nowadays, but at the time people had very little understanding of mental illness. In the past, hysterics had been persecuted, often locked up, or burned as witches because their unusual and sometimes frightening behaviour was attributed to the presence of demons. Even Charcot thought that hysterics, and good hypnotic subjects, suffered from a genetic weakness in the brain. For him, the cause of hysteria had to be purely physical because he was a strict mechanist. He also thought that only hysterics could be hypnotized. Freud had other ideas and began to consider whether hypnosis could be used as a therapy.

Freud began his own private practice as a neuropathologist in 1886, concentrating on the use of hypnosis. His first patient, Frau Emmy von N, suffered from compulsive movements of her face and neck and uncontrollable urges to shout and make odd noises. Nowadays we would recognize these as classic symptoms of Tourette's syndrome – an illness with a neurological basis.

Two main methods of treatment were currently in use with 'neurotic' patients: electrotherapy and hypnosis.

ELECTROTHERAPY

This involved local electrical stimulation of the skin and muscles. Freud considered this method to be useless and said that when it *did* seem to work it was only because of the power of suggestion. In other words, he was once again stating that mental processes could affect physical symptoms.

HYPNOSIS

New research was beginning to suggest that this could work on 'normal' people too. Being susceptible to hypnosis was no longer regarded as a sign of brain damage or genetic weakness. Hypnosis was the first method of treatment for patients with neurotic problems that held Freud's interest.

Freud met Breuer at the Institute of Physiology in 1880, when Breuer was also carrying out research. They became close friends and Breuer helped him with advice and finances, and also passed some of his patients on to him. Unlike other people in the medical profession, who poured scorn on the idea, Breuer was already using hypnosis to help hysterical patients. Eventually, both Freud and Breuer were working mainly with hysterical patients. The two men exchanged ideas and eventually agreed to publish some of their findings together. This was the joint work *Studies On Hysteria*, of which Breuer was the main author.

This book explains how hysteria can be caused by psychological as well as physical events. When the cause was psychological the patient could not remember it at all, even if they tried to. Freud realized that banishing traumatic or threatening memories from the **conscious mind** in this way involved some sort of conflict within the mind between the part that wanted to express an unpleasant emotion and the part that wanted to shut it away because it was too awful to contemplate.

Freud suggested that this banishing process involved an active mechanism. He called this **repression,** and he saw it as being both compulsive and completely unconscious. The process that prevents the unconscious, repressed ideas from being released he called **resistance.**

Insight

It is important to grasp the difference between repression, which is the process of banishing unpleasant or undesirable feelings and experiences to the unconscious mind, and **resistance**, which is the unconscious process that then prevents them from being released.

Freud suggested that the repressed emotion was rather like a mental boil, unable to discharge its toxic contents, and so giving rise instead to neurotic symptoms. In the case of hysteria, these symptoms became physical and expressed the patient's trauma in a symbolic physical form; hence the term **conversion hysteria**.

Insight

Freud cited a case which provides an example of how repression can be expressed in a symbolic, physical form, where a boy's hand froze when his mother asked him to sign a divorce document that denounced his father.

In 1886, Freud gave a lecture on male hysteria to the Vienna Society of Physicians. He was already being looked upon with scorn because of his interest in Charcot's ideas. This new outrage – the very idea that men could suffer from hysteria – met with a fresh wave of hostility. When he dared to describe some cases of hysteria in men there was outrage. One top surgeon remarked that because the word hysteria referred to the uterus, it was obviously impossible for a man to be hysterical. Interestingly, such irrational and extreme denial of Freud's new ideas seems rather neatly to demonstrate repression at work: his ideas were disturbing and therefore both they and their perpetrator needed to be banished!

Freud began to realize that his ideas were always going to be unconventional and that he would have to get used to this type of reaction. It would certainly not be the only occasion on which his ideas were ridiculed. Gradually, he accepted that if he wanted to publish his findings he was bound to meet with hostile reactions.

The very idea that men could suffer from hysteria!

Nineteenth-century scientific and moral thinking

In order to avoid thinking that a lot of Freud's ideas were rather ludicrous and obsessive, it is important to try and understand his work within the context of the times in which he lived.

▶ *The mechanistic view in science made it difficult to look at the way in which a person's mind and ideas can affect their behaviour.*

▶ *Great arguments were going on between scientists and religious thinkers, which largely began with the work of Charles Darwin.*

▶ *The prudish attitude people had towards sex made it difficult to study or discuss anything sexual in a scientific way.*

▶ *The system was patriarchal and men still tended to think they were naturally superior to women.*

Scientific thinking in Freud's day followed the rules of **positivism**, an approach that limits knowledge to things which are directly observable. This goes hand in hand with the mechanistic and deterministic approaches that were so popular at the time – you describe the facts of what you can experience and observe. Anything else is not science. Positivists try to make general scientific laws about the ways in which phenomena are related. This approach began in the natural sciences and spread into philosophy.

Insight

Positivism is a philosophy which limits knowledge to that which is based on actual sense experience. It attempts to affirm theories by strict scientific investigation.

Freud struggled with trying to apply positivism to the way the mind worked. This proved to be tricky, because thoughts, feelings, fantasies and moods are **abstract** in their nature rather than **concrete**. This means that they only exist in thought rather than in solid matter and are therefore hard to observe. Most psychologists took the positivist stance, but **psychiatry** – the study and treatment of mental illnesses – was also developing, as people became interested in the workings of the mind and what could go wrong with it. It was hard to explain these illnesses by means of conventional medicine and mechanistic thinking. People were beginning to understand that psychiatric problems might be rooted in events such as traumatic experiences, and were not always merely an indication of a malfunction in the physical body. This seems obvious to us today, but in Freud's time it was a new way of thinking.

There are probably two main reasons for Freud's insistence upon the positivist stance. Firstly, it was in keeping with the way he was trained as a scientist and the thinking of tutors whom he had admired and respected at university. Secondly, it protected him because it gave him academic respectability. Many of his ideas were so unusual that he needed this credibility in order to carry on with his work. Interestingly, the very name he chose to give his new ideas – psychoanalysis – shows that he wanted his work to be seen as scientific and painstaking.

CHARLES DARWIN

Charles Darwin was the official naturalist on board a ship called the HMS *Beagle*, which went on a world voyage from 1831 to 1836. During this voyage, he accumulated lots of scientific data that led to the formulation of a revolutionary new biological theory – the Theory of Evolution. This caused great uproar when his work *On the Origin of Species* was published in 1859. Darwin's theory of evolution says that:

▶ *the animals and plants that we see today have all descended from an original, simple life form*
▶ *this process depends on 'natural selection' – successful species tend to survive and therefore pass on their genes*
▶ *accidental variations in the genes lead to new species gradually evolving, and unsuccessful variations die out.*

Darwin's ideas were shattering because they were a direct challenge to the traditional religious stories in the Bible, which said that God had created all the species fully formed from the beginning. Man occupied a privileged position in the natural order – he was different from all the animals, because God had given him an immortal soul. Darwin's theories suggested that man had not been specially created by God – he had evolved as a result of a long, slow process, automatically following a natural law. He was different from other animals only in the degree of structural complexity. In addition, man was not a finished product, designed according to a perfect divine plan – he was capable of evolving further. This meant that man was a suitable subject for scientific study, and the huge range of complex human behaviour could be shown to follow scientific principles. Many people were strongly opposed to Darwin's theory because it went against their religious convictions. Others used his ideas to support their own theories about man and his societies. Like Darwin, Freud challenged traditional thinking and met with great opposition.

HELMHOLTZ

There had been huge advances in the field of physics as well as biology. One very important development during the nineteenth century was the formulation of the principle of conservation of energy, put forward by Helmholtz. This principle states that the total amount of energy in any physical system is always constant. Matter can be changed, but never destroyed, so that when energy is moved from one place it must always reappear in another. The Helmholtz principle was applied to various branches of physics, such as thermodynamics and electromagnetism, which began to change the world in all kinds of hugely important ways, for example in the introduction of electrical technology. Biology was quick to take on board the new idea as well, and in 1874 Brücke wrote a book which explained that all living organisms, including human beings, are essentially energy systems, to which the principle of the conservation of energy applies. Because Freud admired Brücke so much he took on board this new 'dynamic physiology' and arrived at the idea that the human personality is also an energy system and that we therefore have 'psychic energy'. The role of the psychologist was therefore to study how this energy works within the psyche. This is really the main basis for Freud's theories of psychoanalysis and he applied the idea in various ways, such as in his theory about sexual repression (see Chapter 3).

PRUDISH ATTITUDES TO SEX

Sex was almost totally unmentionable in the late nineteenth century throughout most of Europe, and it certainly wasn't a topic for discussion in genteel circles. Young girls were not usually taught the facts of life and frequently their first menstruation was a very traumatic event. It seems hardly surprising, therefore, that a lot of Freud's patients, particularly the women, had sexual hang-ups.

Nevertheless, people were naturally interested in sex, and so a sort of duality of attitude existed. This can be seen, for example, in contemporary novels that tended to discuss sexual issues in evasive, coded ways. Cheap newspaper scandals involving sexual exploits were also highly popular, and prostitution was a thriving business.

Everyone is familiar with the traditional image of the stern nineteenth-century patriarch. He ruled his family with a rod of iron, beating the children mercilessly and throwing the servants out on the street when they tiresomely got pregnant by him. Obviously, these images are exaggerated stereotypes, but the man was certainly always the undisputed boss within the family and men held all the most important positions in society – all Freud's tutors and all the people he looked up to were men. Even in the history books and the myths and legends he was taught at school practically all the heroic figures were male. By contrast, women tended to lead very restricted, boring lives, revolving around childrearing and domestic affairs. This, in combination with the strong taboos about sex, meant that women's psychology was as yet very poorly understood.

Some of Freud's ideas seem very sexist to modern people, but we have to remember that this type of attitude was prevalent at the time, and to his credit Freud was one of the pioneers in encouraging people to think about women in a new light. Women were normally seen as intellectually inferior, but Freud developed a very close relationship with his youngest daughter Anna and greatly encouraged her intellectual development and what he saw to be masculine traits in her personality. Obviously he regarded her as an interesting and intelligent human being, but he couldn't quite make the leap to accepting that the positive traits he admired in her could equally well be feminine ones.

Freud's first ideas about the unconscious

THE CASE OF ANNA O

While they were working closely together, Breuer told Freud about the interesting case history of a patient of his – the case of 'Anna O'. This was to be another hugely important step in the development of Freud's theories that led to the idea of psychoanalysis. Anna was a young woman of 21 who suffered from a bewildering variety of symptoms. She had a nervous cough, speech problems, paralysis of her right arm and neck and also had hallucinations. Her hallucinations would gradually get worse through the day until in the evening she fell into a strange trance. While in this state she would mumble odd words.

Anna had recently nursed her father night and day until he died. This traumatic experience seemed to have triggered her illness and she began to refuse food. She also had strange fantasies and mood swings and several times attempted to kill herself. No physical cause could be found for all these strange symptoms and Breuer made a diagnosis of hysteria.

When Anna fell into her evening trance state she would begin to explain her daytime fantasies to Breuer. She called these sessions 'chimney sweeping' or 'the talking cure'. Breuer found that if he repeated words back to her in this trance state then she would describe her hallucinations to him. This made her a little better briefly, but then fresh symptoms would arise.

Sometimes Anna would recall an emotional event that shed light on a particular symptom. For example, after she had been refusing to drink for some time, she spontaneously recalled seeing a woman drink from a glass that a dog had just drunk from. Recalling her feeling of disgust at seeing this incident allowed her to start drinking again. Breuer discovered that when each symptom was traced back to its origin and Anna could describe the original incident to him in as much detail as possible, the symptom would then disappear. The origin of each symptom would turn out to be a forgotten traumatic event. While Anna was actually discussing the trauma her symptoms became very severe.

Breuer also used hypnosis to gain further insights into Anna's problems. His method of curing symptoms by releasing suppressed traumatic memories became known as the **cathartic method,** and the release of repressed emotions was called **abreaction.** So, instead of using hypnosis simply to implant suggestions, hypnosis was being used to unearth past traumas that would then shed light on, and hopefully cure, hysterical symptoms. Freud and Breuer hoped that eventually they could show that all neurotic symptoms could be treated in this way.

Insight

The cathartic method is a method of therapy involving the freeing of repressed emotions. The actual freeing of the emotions is called abreaction. This involves becoming conscious of, and often reliving, traumatic events in order to lessen their emotional impact.

However, there was a snag, because eventually Anna became very dependent on Breuer and fell in love with him. She began telling people she was carrying his child and developed a phantom pregnancy. This was potentially very dangerous for Breuer – he was a married man and such a scandal could be very damaging to his career. He ended the therapy sessions with Anna and later on refused to accept Freud's theories about hidden sexual problems underlying neurosis. Remarkably, Anna must have recovered eventually from her illness because she was later able to lead a fulfilling life as a social worker and feminist. Her real name was Bertha Pappenheim.

STUDIES ON HYSTERIA

In 1895, when Freud and Breuer together published *Studies On Hysteria*, their work presented some rather radical new ideas:

▶ *Negative mental processes can directly affect the physical body and lead to a diseased state. Any traumatic memory that is painful, frightening or shameful in some way can do this.*
▶ *These negative memories remain active in the unconscious mind and can alter a person's behaviour. We cannot get rid of them unless they are recalled, i.e. brought back into the conscious mind.*
▶ *The banishment of unpleasant memories to the unconscious requires an active process operating at an unconscious level.*

This is the process that Freud called repression, the 'first mechanism of defence', and the idea is one of the cornerstones of psychoanalytic thinking.

▶ *The repressed emotional energy or **affect** is converted into hysterical symptoms. These can be permanently erased by abreaction, when the original trauma is relived and gone over in detail.*

▶ *A symptom is often overdetermined, which means that it actually has more than one root cause. This makes therapy more difficult.*

▶ *Symptoms often proved to be symbolic, for example a pain in the heart area when a person had a 'broken heart'.*

Insight

The word 'affect' is used in psychology to suggest an emotion, especially an emotion attached to an idea. 'Affective science' studies emotion and 'affective displays' are such things as facial expression, body posture and so on.

Early on, Freud thought that all repressed emotions were associated with traumatic events that the patient wanted to forget. Nowadays, the idea of uncovering the original trauma and allowing the patient to express the accompanying emotion is still used in the treatment of people suffering post-traumatic stress disorder, for example after an accident. Later, Freud extended his definition of repression to include suppression of instinctive impulses that the patient had been unable to express. For example, one of his female patients was unable to leave her room or even have a visitor without having to urinate several times. Freud linked this back to a trip to the theatre when she had experienced a high degree of sexual arousal when she was strongly attracted to a man.

Freud soon found that some of his patients were very resistant to all this unravelling, and he discovered that there was a constant theme underlying all their cases – one of sexual hang-ups. This was hardly surprising really, given that most of Freud's patients were middle-class women, and women's sexuality was so little understood at that time. But the link between all his cases led

Freud to decide that practically all resistance was sexual in origin – the result of unconscious denial of a forbidden sexual wish. He put forward a thesis that at the bottom of every case of hysteria there lay buried sexual experiences. These were rooted in the earliest years of childhood, but they could be brought to light by psychoanalysis. Freud was so impressed by his own discovery that he described it as a *caput Nili* (source of the Nile) of neuropathology.

Freud decided that in many cases the trauma that had apparently caused a neurosis was too trivial to be the real underlying cause. In these cases he suggested that the unveiled trauma actually harked back to a still earlier trauma, which was invariably of a sexual nature. He did recognize that other emotions could come into play, for example a constriction in the throat could be caused by someone being unable to 'swallow' an insult. But for many years his emphasis was very strongly on the sexual theory. This was probably because sexual impulses are strongly tied in with measurable physiological responses as well as with strong emotional reactions, so this gave Freud a 'scientific' basis for his theories. Without this basis he suggested that he would feel uncomfortable in his explorations of the psyche.

Breuer disagreed with this huge sexual emphasis and there was soon a parting of the ways. This was probably partly because Breuer had been so embarrassed when Anna had developed such a strong sexual attachment to him. One can almost hear Freud saying, 'I rest my case!' But Breuer felt compelled to reject Freud's ideas and so Freud had to continue his research on his own. He soon discovered more and more cases of repressed sexual memories, frequently involving childhood abuse by parents – most often involving fathers and daughters. Eventually, Freud came to realize that many of these cases were actually fantasies representing events that the patient had wished, or perhaps feared might happen. Such fantasies gradually became indistinguishable from reality in the person's mind. There may also have been an element of people obligingly producing what the therapist wanted to hear.

Freud slowly abandoned hypnotism and developed a new technique called the 'pressure technique'. The patient relaxed on a couch and the analyst pressed on his or her forehead, announcing that memories would now be recalled. This method made the analyst into rather an authoritative figure and Freud later abandoned this too.

THINGS TO REMEMBER

▶ *Freud trained originally in medicine.*

▶ *After working with Charcot he became interested in hysteria and hypnosis.*

▶ *Freud began his own private practice as a neuropathologist in 1886, using electrotherapy and hypnosis to treat patients.*

▶ *The commonly accepted scientific view at this time was the mechanistic view.*

▶ *Many of Freud's ideas were regarded with suspicion and cynicism by other scientists.*

▶ *Freud became interested in the unconscious while working with Josef Breuer.*

▶ *Working with his own patients Freud developed the idea that all neurotic symptoms were caused by repressed sexual experiences.*

▶ *Freud's work was gradually suggesting to him the existence of conflict between two parts of the mind. This conflict led to the process that Freud called resistance. It was ideas like this that gradually led Freud to his discoveries about the unconscious.*

3

The beginnings of psychoanalysis

In this chapter you will learn:
- *key features of Freud's emerging theories of psychoanalysis*
- *some basic elements of the psychoanalytical technique*
- *the background to Freud's first attempts at psychoanalysis.*

The crucial decade

Freud's theories about psychoanalysis had already begun to evolve during the time he worked with Breuer. During the decade centred around the turn of the nineteenth century, he developed most of the major ideas about the development and functioning of the human psyche that were to become psychoanalysis. Following *Studies On Hysteria*, Freud entered a period of huge intellectual activity during which he produced several more important works. In 1896 he wrote various papers outlining a new theory about how neuroses arose, which he called the 'seduction theory' (see below). This work was followed in 1900 by his important book *The Interpretation of Dreams*, and *Three Essays on the Theory of Sexuality* was published in 1905.

It was during this period that psychoanalysis really began to emerge as a way of studying the psyche, a clinical method and a developmental theory. All these aspects were interrelated and inspired by Freud's experiences with his own patients and by an extensive analysis of his own psyche, based largely on dream analysis. He was gradually moving away from the strictly mechanistic, empirical science that he had been trained in, and his work took on a much more introspective slant. Many of the changes in his theoretical thinking reflect his significant struggle to understand himself. However, he always insisted that his work was scientifically based and got very defensive if anybody suggested otherwise. It is particularly interesting to read his letters to Fliess during this period, because they reflect many of the tensions that he must have been feeling.

The repression of sexual ideas

At first Freud thought that neurotic symptoms were always caused by traumatic events. Following his early determinist training, he hoped to prove that neuroses were always physical in origin. In an early study called *Project for a Scientific Psychology*, he even tried to link neurotic symptoms with actual anatomy and physiology. Eventually he abandoned this line of research however, when case studies such as that of Anna O led him to the important discovery that these symptoms can also be caused by repressed sexual urges. Freud still adhered firmly to scientific principles, saying that these sexual urges are instinctive and represent a basic biological drive. Because this drive is a form of energy it cannot be destroyed when it is repressed. It still exists intact, in a repressed form in the unconscious, from where it exerts an influence on the conscious mind and can give rise to dysfunctional behaviour and neurotic thinking.

Freud saw the human psyche as constantly striving towards a peaceful state. This meant that any strong emotions, either positive or negative, were seen as unpleasant and therefore needed to be got rid of in order to release tension. This idea was later named the 'nirvana principle'. Nirvana is a Buddhist idea meaning 'blowing out', as in blowing out a candle. It refers to the idea that the goal of life is to enter a state of nothingness: in this empty state a person becomes one with the life force of the universe, or 'prana'. Freud wasn't really referring to this transcendental bliss state – he simply used the word nirvana to refer to a state where there is no psychic tension. He came to believe that the most potent and overriding source of negative feelings was the lack of a fulfilling sex life. The assumption was therefore that 'normal' people, without neurotic symptoms, must have a fantastic sex life that provided them with the necessary release of tension needed to attain the desired nirvana state.

Freud now claimed confidently that all neurotic symptoms are caused by traumatic sexual experiences, often in early childhood. Sexual satisfaction in adulthood was the key to happiness and emotional balance. This idea became central to psychoanalytic theory, and Freud remained adamant about it for a long time. We must remember that because of the times in which he lived there was a prevailing prudish attitude towards any mention of sex. Moreover, there was no proper means of birth control. This meant that once your family was complete you had to abstain, or furtively seek satisfaction elsewhere. It is likely that this social attitude led to more people having neurotic symptoms that were connected to sexual repression. Most of the patients who came to Freud were neurotic, middle-class women who suffered with problems of this sort.

The seduction theory

As a result of early case studies, Freud focused more and more on the influence of sexual experience. He claimed that the key to all neuroses was, in fact, the suppressed memory of an early childhood seduction by an adult. But he realized that not everyone who had experienced sexual abuse in childhood later developed neurotic symptoms. His explanation for this was that the experience only led to a neurosis if it was suppressed. It then festered in the unconscious, only to re-emerge at puberty as a neurosis. If, on the other hand, a person retained full conscious awareness of what had happened, then no neurosis would develop.

After a while Freud abandoned this theory for several reasons. The whole picture was suspiciously common – could it be that some of his patients were inventing the whole thing to fit in with their doctor's theory? He also realized that some of his siblings showed neurotic symptoms – surely his own father was not guilty of incest? Freud's letters to Fliess at this time show that he really agonized over this and eventually concluded that it could not possibly be the case. Eventually, he had a better idea and decided that some of the 'memories' that patients came up with were in fact fantasies. These arose in order to fulfil hidden desires.

This was an important breakthrough – it had dawned on Freud that fantasies could actually be more important than real events in our struggle to understand the human psyche. During analysis, people were coming up with fantasies that were based on instinctive urges. Freud described an incident in his own childhood when he had glimpsed his mother naked and had felt the first stirrings of sexual desire. Perhaps some of the seduction scenes that his patients were describing to him could actually be fantasies based on similar early erotic experiences? This new idea gradually led Freud to develop his theories about infantile sexuality and dreams. Until then people had tended to think that children were totally devoid of sexual urges. Once again Freud was producing new and uncomfortable ideas.

From this time onwards psychoanalysis became more about exploring this secret inner world than trying to unravel a neat causal chain of actual events that had led to the formation of neurotic problems. Freud developed these new ideas in two main ways – through extensive studies of dreams, and in theories about how sexuality develops throughout childhood.

Insight

Later on Freud said that dreams were often **overdetermined**, being influenced by recent events, past traumas and unconscious wishes.

The pressure technique

Freud seems to have given up using hypnosis completely before
he really began to develop his theories of psychoanalysis. For
quite a while after this he used the pressure technique. He would
sit behind his patient, who was lying on a couch, and when the
patient encountered a resistance to talking about something, he
would apply pressure either to the forehead or to either side of the
head. This pressure, he explained, would overcome the resistance.
Freud became very keen on this method for a while, and declared
that it could unblock resistance in every case. Interestingly, it
often gave rise to visual images rather than a fresh flow of words,
and frequently patients would recall past scenes that they had
previously completely forgotten. These scenes would then unblock
a fresh flow of words about what had happened.

Sometimes these scenes, or isolated words that the patient came up
with, would lead to fresh insights into the problem he and his patient
were working on. But sometimes nothing happened, or the scenes
and words that came up would seem to be irrelevant. Usually Freud
would then apply pressure again, and try to get the patient to come
up with more images and words. In this way he helped people to
build up chains of related ideas which sometimes did seem to make
sense and help a person to understand what was bothering them.

For example, one patient came up with a single word, concierge,
which made no sense to her at all. By pressing repeatedly Freud
got her to say 'night-gown', 'bed', 'town' and 'farm-cart'. When
they put all this together the patient recalled an entire incident
from when she was ten years old and her 12-year-old sister had
gone completely mad one night. She had been overpowered by a
concierge, tied up and taken into town in a hand-cart to an asylum.
After further probing, Freud discovered that she and this sister had
shared not only a bed, but also sexual abuse from the same man.

Freud gradually began to understand that, as with hypnosis,
there was a snag to using the pressure method. In both cases

the analyst was put in a position of authority and the patient was not in control. Soon he realized that using the pressure method also meant that the analyst's voice could interrupt the patient's flow of thought. Even worse, he recognized a tendency for the analyst actually to plant ideas that might not have been there to begin with.

You will remember!

The free-association technique

Freud therefore developed a modified version of the pressure technique. The patient was encouraged to relax on the couch and then simply feel free to voice whatever thoughts drifted into his or her mind without censorship. The role of the analyst had now changed – ideally he was there simply to guide the patient. In practice it was not always easy to retain this passive role. This new method – one of the keystones of psychoanalysis – is called the **free-association technique**. The idea behind it was that only the patient could really discover the key to the neurosis – this method put the patient back in control of what went on. However, Freud discovered that when the patient got close to the root cause of the neurosis resistance was likely to occur.

Insight

The free-association technique is still used today by analysts. The idea is not to have any pre-planned conversation, or to look for specific answers, but rather to explore in an unstructured, intuitive kind of way. This can often lead to unearthing things which are meaningful and important to the patient.

From 1894 until 1900 Freud developed many of the theories that we now see as being central to psychoanalysis. He carefully examined and analysed the unconscious mechanisms, such as repression and resistance, that he saw underlying neurotic symptoms. Freud coined the term psychoanalysis in 1896. The main theories that he was developing during this period were connected with:

▶ *dream analysis*
▶ *slips of the tongue*
▶ *infantile sexuality.*

Transference

Freud also became interested in what he called **transference**. Sometimes, even after weeks of work using the pressure technique, the patient would still become blocked and the analysis would seem to be going nowhere. In this case Freud suggested three possibilities:

▶ *there was really nothing further to be unearthed*
▶ *the patient had come up against a resistance that could only be shifted later on*

▶ *or – and he saw this as the worst possibility – the patient's relationship with the doctor was somehow getting in the way. Freud believed that this problem arose sooner or later in every analysis.*

Freud began to use the word transference to describe the emotional feelings the patient developed towards the analyst. This could involve either positive or negative emotions. For example, the patient may actually fall in love with the therapist, as Anna O did with Breuer. Alternatively, the patient might become very hostile towards the analyst. Freud decided that this is because the patient is beginning to attribute to the analyst ideas and attitudes that actually belong to other emotionally significant people, in particular the parents.

Insight

Transference is about redirecting feelings and desires, especially those that have been repressed since childhood. Think of the type of complicated emotional response that can happen when someone says, or does, something that reminds you of sensitive issues from your past.

Freud saw three main ways in which an emotional block could happen:

▶ *The patient feels he or she has been neglected or insulted by the doctor. This can easily be overcome by discussion in most cases.*
▶ *The patient feels he or she is in danger of becoming too dependent on the doctor, or even falling in love with him. This is harder to deal with and can give rise to fresh hysterical symptoms.*
▶ *Transference is occurring as the patient begins to project the upsetting ideas he or she is unearthing onto the doctor. Freud says that transference is a very common occurrence, for example one patient suddenly announced that she wanted Freud to kiss her. This, he maintained, proved to be a repressed desire from an incident that had occurred years earlier with another man. Her refusal to recognize this blocked the course of the analysis.*

Whenever transference occurred, then analysis of the transference itself would finally unblock the problem. But this led Freud to a fresh problem, because anything the analyst did, such as a physical gesture or contact, might inadvertently reinforce the transference. This meant that eventually Freud rarely touched his patients at all, and was very careful about the way he greeted them and so on.

Nowadays it is accepted as normal for some degree of transference to take place during the course of psychoanalytic treatment – in fact, it is part of the healing process as the patient directs feelings of love or hostility towards the analyst. This can actually be very helpful because it recreates the original problem in miniature. Freud called this a transference neurosis. The advantage is that unconscious feelings are now out in the open and can be examined and hopefully dealt with properly.

The term 'transference' is nowadays extended to mean the patient's whole emotional attitude to the analyst, and it is recognized that the current relationship between analyst and patient is often hugely important. Freud himself recognized this and gradually realized that it was impossible to maintain the totally clinical type of relationship with a patient that he had initially thought to be essential. Although he saw transference as a great nuisance, he began to recognize its importance and eventually realized that a counter-transference often occurred, where the therapist also has emotional reactions towards the patient. This, he explained, was because of the influence of the patient on the unconscious feelings of the therapist. Freud suggested that it was important to recognize this process and overcome it.

Freud's self-analysis

Freud's own self-analysis was to prove very important in the evolution of psychoanalysis, and it forms the core of his book *The Interpretation of Dreams*. In 1896 Freud's father died. For the next three years Freud went through a period of gloom, while he struggled to come to terms with conflicting feelings thrown up by his father's death. Freud later termed a mixed attitude such as this 'ambivalence'. On the one hand he felt love and respect towards his father, and on the other he felt hostility and guilt. Freud had a lot of responsibilities by this time. He had six children, and his wife, mother and some of his sisters were also dependent on him. His father's death must have left him feeling very alone in the world and he laid great emphasis on the trauma a man felt at this time. This was all part of Freud's belief in the huge importance of the male as the figurehead of the family.

However, his period of darkness, one that we now know to be common at around the age of 40, did have its plus side in that it threw him into a period of intensive self-analysis that was to prove very productive. He began to realize that he had long repressed feelings of resentment and rage towards his father and that these feelings were now emerging in the form of feelings of shame and impotence. This revelation led him to examine his childhood memories, his dreams, and slips of the tongue which shed telling light on his unconscious world.

Freud recalled that he had often fantasized in his youth that his older half-brother Philip was his real father. (You will remember that Philip was in fact about the same age as his mother.) Eventually, he grasped the horrible truth of this fantasy – that he had actually had a death wish against his real father, because he was a rival for his mother's attention. This revelation was to become one of the main bases for his **Oedipus complex** theory (see Chapter 7).

Insight

The Oedipus complex is about the desire the child has to sexually possess the parent of the opposite sex, while excluding the parent of the same sex.

Freud also realized that unconscious childhood memories often surfaced in adult dreams. For example, it was in a dream that he recalled having had sexual feelings towards his mother when he caught sight of her naked when he was a child. The importance of repressed childhood memories, which emerge in dreams and fantasies, also became central to psychoanalytic theory.

Freud had already found that dreams played a very important role in his analysis of neurotic patients. As he encouraged people to free-associate, they often mentioned their dreams, and the images in them would usually set off further trains of thought. Now he began to record and analyse his own dreams, and decided that they, like waking daydreams, always represented some sort of wish fulfilment. It was at this point that he decided to write *The Interpretation of Dreams*.

This book, arguably Freud's most important work, contains analyses of many of Freud's own dreams. They include the famous dream of 'Irma's Injection', which is a very important dream in the history of psychoanalysis, because it was the first one of his own dreams that he submitted to methodical, public analysis. In this dream he and some other doctors are examining Irma, a patient of his, and discussing various symptoms that are plaguing her. Freud's analysis suggests that the dream was allowing his unconscious to express some guilt and worry that he was feeling deep down about his partial failure in treating this patient and transfer the blame onto the other doctors.

He was always as objective as possible when working with his own dreams, trying to view himself as he would a client. In the book he explains that dreams have a double nature – a **manifest content** – which is what the dream appears to be about, and a **latent content** – which is the dream's true, hidden meaning.

By the time the book was published in 1900 Freud was much more confident about his theories and had laid down the main foundations – both the main techniques and the theoretical framework – of psychoanalytic thinking. He was using two main approaches with his clients, which are still used today:

▶ The free-association method. *Freud encouraged his patients to make connections between mental images and hidden memories. By talking about these he found that he could lead the person deeper and deeper into the unconscious.*

▶ Dream analysis. *Freud found that dreams were a very revealing way of accessing what lay in the unconscious.*

The Interpretation of Dreams was slow in gaining any recognition. Most scientists at the time dismissed dreams as being unimportant ramblings of the sleeping mind, so yet again Freud was ahead of his time. It took eight years to sell the original 600 copies printed in 1900: the scientific journals ignored it completely for the first year and a half, and critics were as damning of his ideas as ever, suggesting they could lead to 'complete mysticism'. By 1910, however, Freud was gaining recognition and the first reprint of the book was made, followed by six more during Freud's lifetime.

The Interpretation of Dreams shows us that Freud was beginning to realize that neurotic symptoms actually occur in all of us, not just in people who are ill. The second important book which bears out this idea, *Psychopathology of Everyday Life*, appeared at the end of Freud's period of withdrawal, in 1901. This book covers the other main discoveries that he made during this period of intense self-analysis – that is, slips of the tongue and similar mistakes in speech and writing. From this point onwards **psychopathology** had entered the arena of so-called 'normal' life. Freud continued to analyse his own unconscious psychic world right up until the end of his life.

Insight

The word psychopathology implies that something is wrong in the psyche, because pathology is the study of bodily disease.

The analysis of Dora

Dora (her real name was Ida Bauer), was an 18-year-old girl whom Freud saw as a client in 1900. The case is interesting for two reasons:

▶ *It is one of the earliest recorded case histories in psychoanalysis and one of the first where dreams were used as the main basis for the analysis. Although the therapy itself was a failure the case was used for years as a classic case study for students.*

▶ *It highlights some possible pitfalls in the psychoanalytic method.*

Dora's father had already been to Freud as a patient, presenting symptoms of syphilis, and he brought Dora along to Freud in order to 'make her see reason' (an interesting statement that may give a clue about the real source of Dora's neurosis). Dora's mother had an obsessive compulsive disorder, constantly cleaning the house, but Dora refused to take on the traditional female role and preferred instead to read a lot and try to educate herself. She was beginning to display typical hysterical symptoms, such as fainting and depression. She had an endless nagging cough and had at times become mute for a while. By the time she came to see Freud she had also threatened suicide.

The story is a complicated one, but the main focus was a tangled web of relationships that existed between Dora's family and another family, referred to as the K family. Dora used to babysit for the young K children and Freud claimed that she had a crush on Frau K, who was also her father's mistress. The two women were certainly close, almost like sisters, but it is not clear whether they actually had a sexual relationship. Meanwhile Frau K's husband, Herr K, who knew all about his wife's affair, had allegedly made sexual advances to Dora since she was 14. When Dora finally told her father what was going on he accused her of having invented the whole thing.

Freud believed Dora's story, but even though Dora vehemently and consistently announced that she hated Herr K, he got it into his head that the root of the problem was that she was secretly in love with him. He even found it hard to understand why she felt revulsion rather than sexual excitement when Herr K pressed his erect penis against her. The more Dora declared her hatred, the more Freud announced that this was clear evidence of repression of her true feelings – even though on one occasion, when Herr K had propositioned her during a walk by a lake, she had slapped him across the face. The more vehement the denial, claimed Freud, the stronger the repression must be. Heads I win, tails you lose.

Eventually, after 11 weeks in therapy, Dora quit. She had been labelled by now as a lesbian, and the analysis certainly did nothing to alter her sexual orientation. However, Freud claimed that she had eventually accepted the idea that she was in love with Herr K. All this really goes to show is how stubborn and persuasive Freud could be once he got the bit between his teeth. He had warned Dora's parents from the outset that therapy was unlikely to be successful, and in fact this proved to be the case. Hardly surprising since Dora's own wishes had not been taken into account – she was not really ill, and she had not asked to be brought for therapy.

Dora finally accepts the idea that she is in love with Herr K.

It was not until 1905 that the Dora case notes appeared, starkly entitled *Fragment of an Analysis of a Case of Hysteria*, in a specialist journal. Although they were used for many years as a case study for students, more recently people have begun to realize that the Dora analysis was really just as much an analysis of Freud himself as of young Dora. Dora herself seems to have been a determined young woman struggling with extremely difficult emotional circumstances and putting up a fight against adults who had as yet limited understanding of women's sexuality and adolescent needs.

THINGS TO REMEMBER

▶ *Early on in the development of psychoanalysis, Freud decided that all neurotic symptoms were caused by sexual experiences.*

▶ *At first he claimed that the key to all neuroses was in fact the suppressed memory of an early childhood seduction by an adult.*

▶ *He developed a new therapeutic technique called the free-association technique. He used mainly free association and dream analysis in his therapy.*

▶ *Freud coined the term psychoanalysis in 1896.*

▶ *Transference refers to emotional attitudes developed by the patient towards the analyst. This can be a two-way process.*

▶ *Freud's mid-life crisis led him to carry out extensive self-analysis, with particular emphasis on dreams.*

▶ *His book* The Interpretation of Dreams *was published in 1900.*

▶ *The analysis of 'Dora' is one of the earliest recorded case histories in psychoanalysis.*

4

The interpretation of dreams

In this chapter you will learn:
- *why dreams are important in psychoanalysis*
- *dream mechanisms and methods of interpretation*
- *Freudian symbols and the origins of dreams.*

Why dreams are important in psychoanalysis

Probably Freud's greatest contribution to modern thinking is his theory of the unconscious. The positivism that was popular in Freud's time claimed that people could gain real knowledge of the world and of themselves, and that we had rational control over both. This sort of attitude was reflected throughout scientific thinking, with its insistence on 'hard facts', and it even permeated psychology. Freud began to realize that such claims are at best delusions, because we are not always aware of what we really think and we are often motivated by unconscious forces within us. He suggested that consciousness actually existed in layers and that there were many psychic processes that went on below the surface, in the world of the unconscious. Dreams were the most immediate and accessible examples of this kind of unconscious thinking – not only did they prove that the unconscious exists, they also provided a means of accessing the information stored there. Freud's book, *The Interpretation of Dreams*, really marks the beginning of psychoanalysis proper, in that it proposes the existence of a dynamic unconscious that begins to form in childhood and affects the behaviour of all of us. It does not, however, live up to its claim that Freud had discovered a scientific method for unravelling the meaning of every dream.

People have always been interested in dreams, but before Freud they tended to think that the dream somehow arose from outside the dreamer, often as a message from the gods. Thus, dreams were often seen as omens or portents of things that were going to happen in the future. Another theory was that dreams were simply meaningless images caused by indigestion! There was already a great deal of literature concerning dreams in Freud's day, but he pulled a whole variety of ideas together. He created the first proper theory of dreams and made them into a respectable topic for scientific study.

Freud had always been very interested in dreams and emphasized their importance in psychoanalysis. In fact, he regarded them as being so important that he said if anyone asked him how to become a psychoanalyst he would tell them to study their own dreams. He regarded his discovery of the importance of dreams as his greatest. Staying at the Schloss Bellevue outside Vienna in the summer of 1895, he had a dream which was the first he was able to interpret as a wish-fulfilment dream. This dream appears in *The Interpretation of Dreams* as 'The Dream of Irma's Injection'. Freud was so excited by his new ideas about dreams that he wrote a letter to Fliess, suggesting that one day a marble plaque would be erected at the Schloss Bellevue, commemorating his monumental revelation. The Schloss Bellevue has since been demolished, but Freud would have been delighted to know that such a plaque was at last placed on a monument on the site in 1977.

Dream analysis, alongside **free association**, became one of the main therapeutic methods in psychoanalysis. As usual, Freud very much emphasized that he was interested in the study of dreams from the scientific viewpoint. In the preface to *The Interpretation of Dreams* he makes this point, saying that in his attempts to explore dream interpretation he does not feel that he has overstepped the boundary of neuropathological science. Once again he was covering his back, in anticipation of the criticism which was bound to come his way from other members of the scientific establishment.

Freud discovered that when patients were free-associating on the couch they quite often spontaneously began to tell him about their own dreams. For Freud, the unconscious contained all the repressed desires that were not accessible to the conscious waking mind – it was impossible to find out what was in the unconscious just by thinking about it. He realized that dreams were one way in which the unconscious could be accessed indirectly.

Dreams became central to psychoanalysis for several reasons:

▶ *They occur during sleep, when the conscious mind relaxes and is off guard. Freud therefore saw dreams as evidence of the unconscious mind at work and proof of its existence. He referred to dreams as being the 'royal road' to deeper understanding of the unconscious.*
▶ *Freud had come to recognize that hypnosis and the pressure method were too authoritarian. He realized that you cannot force a person to understand what is going on in their unconscious. Only by the new methods of dream analysis and free association could one really begin to understand the symbolism involved in neurotic symptoms.*
▶ *While Freud was busy working out his main theories about dreams he was also developing ideas about infantile sexuality. He was convinced that dreams are often concerned with sexual issues from very early childhood. These problems could only be resolved through dream analysis and free association.*
▶ *Freud saw dreams as symbolic wish fulfilments of desires that have been repressed. By exploring the hidden desire symbolized in a dream one could, therefore, begin to unravel the problem.*

Dreams as wish fulfilment

People have always tended to see some of their dreams as wish-fulfilment fantasies. We use phrases like 'in your dreams' or 'not even in my wildest dreams'. Freud carried this idea further and announced that dreams were almost always driven by the need to fulfil a repressed wish. So dreams are very similar to daydreams or stories in which we end up achieving our heart's desire.

In its simplest form, a dream directly expresses a wish. For example, Freud describes the dream of a young mother, who was cut off from society for weeks while she nursed a child through an infectious illness. In her dream she met lots of well-known authors and had fascinating conversations with them. When Freud's little girl Anna was sick and not allowed any food, she dreamed of strawberries, omelette and pudding. This type of direct wish-fulfilment dream is common in small children: Freud said that analysis of the dreams of small children will always prove them to be fulfilments of wishes that arose the day before the dream and were not fulfilled.

Freud also recorded dreams of his own of this type, for example he noticed that if he had been eating salty food such as sardines or olives then he would dream about drinking water. Another drinking dream revealed a deeper wish fulfilment, when he dreamed that the water he was drinking was contained in an Etruscan urn that he no longer owned but regretted having parted with.

Freud saw dreaming largely as a form of regression to childhood and the instinctual forces and images that dominate this time of our lives. As we grow up we soon learn that not all our desires can be instantly fulfilled. The inhibitions that are imposed on us by parents and caretakers gradually become internalized and so the forbidden wishes become unconscious. Freud called this process 'censorship', and he thought that dreams were mostly disguised manifestations of infantile sexual urges that had been repressed.

Strawberries, omelette and pudding.

Because these urges were unacceptable they were suppressed and so the dream – like the neurotic symptom – is a censored way of expressing what has been buried. According to Freud, recent events and desires in a person's life play only a minor part in dreams – they usually appear only if they somehow trigger one of the early repressed desires. It is hard to see why this should be the case and in this respect Freud's ideas differ from modern theories about dreams, where recent and current events are very important. Freud believed that the wishes represented in dreams were almost always infantile ones, even when the infantile desire is not at first suspected. This idea harks back to, and reinforces, his original idea that hysterical symptoms had their roots in early childhood trauma.

For Freud, dreams were neurotic symptoms. The fact that everyone has dreams made it clear to him that psychoanalysis was relevant to all of us, not only those suffering from psychiatric illness.

Dreams, he said, allow the impossible to happen, and set aside the inhibitions of waking life. During sleep, forbidden wishes rise from the unconscious, where they are normally kept under control during waking hours. As they attempt to come into the conscious mind, the dream censor in the brain monitors them and decides that they have disturbing content and therefore must be suppressed for fear they disturb the sleeper. Dreams are then created in order to express the hidden wishes in a disguised form, so that the person can go on sleeping. Dreams are thus seen by Freud as guardians, allowing us to sleep peacefully. He remarked that they expose our hidden urges to the extent that anyone who behaved the same way when awake as they did in their dreams would be seen as insane. He certainly has a point there!

In cases where it seemed impossible to unravel a hidden wish fulfilment, Freud cunningly used two possible explanations:

▶ *The patient is in a state of negative transference to the analyst. He or she is deliberately producing awkward dreams in order to trip up the analyst and disprove his theories. For example, Freud cites a case where a barrister friend dreamed that he had lost all his cases. Freud and he had been rivals at school and Freud had always beaten him, so in the dream he is identifying with Freud and hoping that he will lose. This means that the dream conceals a hidden wish fulfilment.*
▶ *The patient is employing mental masochism – the dream is satisfying a masochistic urge, which is in itself a form of wish fulfilment.*

These two explanations could perhaps be seen as further examples of Freud's own stubbornness when he wanted to prove a theory! It seems strange that Freud so obstinately stuck to his theory that dreams are mainly about repressed infantile wishes. This view has often been criticized as being **reductionist,** and in fact many of the dreams Freud discusses are clearly about adult needs and problems, for example the dream of 'Irma's Injection', which was expressing anxiety about his own competence as a doctor. He did admit eventually that there are various types of dreams that do not fit in with his theory:

▶ *Some dreams need no interpretation – when we are hungry we dream of food; when we are hard-up we dream of finding piles of money.*
▶ *There are traumatic dreams, in which we endlessly and directly relive things like the horror of an accident. During and after the First World War, Freud had experience with shock and trauma victims who often relived recent ghastly wartime experiences in their dreams. This led Freud to question his earlier insistence that dreams were always wish fulfilment and always harked back to childhood.*
▶ *Some dreams have nightmare content, or bring up huge feelings of anxiety. It is difficult to see how these can always be masked wish fulfilments.*

Dream mechanisms

It is obvious that some simple dreams can be seen as wish-fulfilment fantasies, but how can one say the same of a nightmare, or an anxiety dream? Freud explained that some nightmares or anxiety dreams appear as a result of dream censor mechanisms having failed, allowing some of the anxiety connected with forbidden impulses to emerge. The sleeper would generally wake up at this point because the censor was no longer allowing peaceful sleep to continue.

MANIFEST AND LATENT MEANINGS

Freud went further and explained that each dream has both a 'manifest' and a 'latent' content. The manifest content of the dream is the part that is consciously remembered; the latent part is the disguised part that is not remembered before analysis.

Insight

You may have noticed that Freud is not being very scientific here. He describes the manifest part of a dream as the part which is consciously remembered. The latent part is *not* consciously remembered before analysis. So surely there is a great risk of suggestive input from the analyst here? (See the case of the Wolf Man in Chapter 10.)

Freud explained that the technique used to uncover the latent content of the dream is exactly the same as the method used in free association. You simply set aside the apparent connections between all the elements of the dream and take each element separately. You then use the free-association technique and collect all the ideas that arise in association with each separate element of the dream. From this material you then arrive at the latent content of the dream. Analysis of the latent content will always show that the dream meaning can be traced back to childhood. The latent content of the dream is the true meaning, and just as with the dreams of small children, it will always represent fulfilment of unsatisfied wishes from the previous day. The manifest content of the dream – i.e. the part that you remember when you wake up in the morning – is merely a disguised fulfilment of repressed wishes.

So anxiety, for example, might only appear in the manifest aspect of the dream, but if the dream is properly interpreted, one will still find a hidden wish fulfilment lurking beneath the apparent meaning of the dream. The latent content of the dream is actually the cause of the dream. Freud proposed two mechanisms at work here:

▶ *the sleeping mind begins to create a dream, based on a wish fulfilment*
▶ *the mind is shocked by the wish and imposes censorship on it causing distortion in the way the wish is allowed to appear in the dream.*

Freud gives an example of this process. One of his patients challenged him, announcing that she had had a dream that was the exact opposite of a wish fulfilment. She dreamt that she wanted to hold a supper party, but various things kept going wrong. There was not enough food. It was Sunday, so she couldn't order more to be delivered. The phone was out of

Her husband preferred plump women.

order … and so on. How could he say that this dream expressed a wish fulfilment?

Freud was cunning. Analysis of the dream revealed a hidden jealously of the friend whom she had been going to invite to the supper party. She was afraid that her husband fancied this friend, but fortunately the friend was skinny, and as her husband preferred plump women she felt reasonably safe. However, she was damned if she wanted to fatten her up with a special supper party! So the dream was, in fact, a disguised fulfilment of a repressed wish.

Other mechanisms

Freud said that the latent content of the dream could only be revealed through dream analysis and free association. The latent aspect of the dream is seen as being the important part because it contains the real meaning, which has been censored. The thought processes of the unconscious brain are irrational and incomplete.

The goal is simply to evade the censor and allow the dream ideas to be expressed somehow. Freud suggested that there were various mechanisms at work that allowed the dream wish to be expressed but in a distorted form:

▶ **Displacement** – *potentially disturbing feelings about a situation are not expressed directly; instead they are associated in the dream with something different but somehow connected. The manifest content of the dream is very different from the latent content, but the associated feelings remain very much the same. This means that the manifest content of the dream can be about apparently trivial events, but associated with powerful feelings that don't necessarily seem appropriate. Conversely, ghastly things can happen in the manifest dream with no accompanying flood of emotion.*

Insight

Displacement is the shifting of emotions attached to one idea onto another idea. Freud was always trying to make his work appear scientific, so he may have borrowed this idea from Newtonian mechanics, where displacement is the difference between the initial position and the final position of an object.

▶ **Condensation** – *here, two or more ideas or images are fused together in the dream. In this way a dream image may have more than one root cause, and much deeper real meanings may lie behind the dream image. So examination of an image in the manifest dream may lead to a whole host of overlapping and related ideas in the latent dream.*

Insight

Condensation is the fusion of two or more ideas – in a dream, or the telling a joke for example. Again, this idea may have been borrowed from science to suggest a scientific basis for Freud's theories (for example, in earth science water vapour condenses onto a cold surface to form water droplets).

▶ **Symbolization** – *dream images or ideas are often symbolic and so secretly represent other things. According to Freud, most dream symbolism is sexual in nature.*

Insight

In Freud's thinking, symbolization is about representing an object or an idea with a different object or idea. This forms a kind of safe disguise: for example a dream cave could symbolize a womb. Jung later argued that Freud's idea of what constituted a symbol was too simplistic and that dream symbols could often have much richer, more complex meanings.

▶ Resistance – *Freud said that we tend to forget dreams because of dream censorship, which still tries to prevent the dream ideas from entering conscious thought.*
▶ Representation – *a process by which thoughts are converted into visual images.*
▶ Dramatization – *Freud observed that dreams are mainly made up of a flow of vivid visual images. These often seem to lack any logical structure with mysterious and seemingly unconnected images, the connections between which can only be discovered during subsequent analysis. This dramatic visual sequence and its underlying meaning is what Freud called 'dramatization'.*
▶ Secondary revision – *here, the dreamer tries to make some sense of the dream as he or she recounts it after waking. As the dream is made into a more coherent 'story', the latent content is often still further disguised.*

Obviously then, by the time the dreamer recalls the dream and relates it to the therapist, a whole host of potential mechanisms have churned into action to disguise the real original meaning. In fact, many of these are mechanisms cunningly put into place by Freud in order to prove his own theory that dreams are fulfilments of infantile sexual fantasies! He says that if we analyse our own dreams, we will be astonished to discover what an unexpectedly great part the experiences and impressions of our early childhood still play in our lives. In dream life, childish wishes and impulses still rule us – even those that are of no use to us whatsoever in our adult lives. This would seem to be true to some extent, and it may sometimes be helpful to unearth these primitive wishes and look at them in the light of adult logic.

There are also other aspects to Freud's ideas about dreams that are just as relevant today. For example, it seems indisputably true that the unconscious often speaks to us in symbols, but it seems likely that this has more to do with the way the unconscious brain works than with furtively censoring hidden desires. It is also true that dreams can reveal our true selves – unmasking our hidden fears and desires – and they are invaluable resources in trying to understand ourselves better.

Methods of dream interpretation

Freud maintained that every dream has a meaning, and that the meaning of the dream is the cause of the dream. He realized that this was not a new idea – even Aristotle saw dreams as the mental activity of the sleeper rather than messages sent by the gods. The mechanistic view tended to lead people to believe that dreams were the meaningless result of physical processes in the sleeping body. Freud disagreed, pointing out that non-scientists had always seen dreams as being full of hidden meaning.

Freud described two methods with which dreams were usually interpreted:

▶ The symbolic method – *for example, Joseph's dream in the bible, where seven fat cattle are followed by seven thin ones that eat them up. This was interpreted symbolically as showing the seven years of famine that would follow seven years of plenty. This method tended to fall down where dreams were very confused and unintelligible.*

▶ The decoding method – *here, one used a fixed interpretation, of the type that is often given in books about dream interpretation. Freud said that this was not scientific because the original interpretation could be wrong.*

Freud discovered that while his patients were relaxing and free associating, they began to tell him about their dreams. He saw their dreams as further symptoms, and the method he used to unravel them was really the same free-association method as he used for other problems. During the process of free association and dream analysis the patient had to be relaxed and feel safe. This meant that two things could happen:

▶ *The patient and analyst could both pay closer attention to what was going on in the patient's thought processes.*
▶ *They were able to remove the critical censor that normally sifts thought processes as they arise.*

In effect, Freud's new method was reversing the critical, repressive attitudes that prevailed in Vienna at the time. He was encouraging people to look at themselves in an uncritical way. Freud helped people to analyse each part of a dream separately; often a painstaking process. In *The Interpretation of Dreams* he analyses many of his own dreams, because he felt that his clients, being 'neuropaths', might have dreams that did not represent the 'norm'. Also, to analyse clients' dreams would often mean exposing a good deal of confidential case history.

Freud gave advice about dream interpretation that is still very helpful today:

▶ *To interpret a dream is hard work and one has to persevere at the task.*
▶ *After working on a dream it should then be left alone – fresh insights may come later.*
▶ *Dreams often occur in groups with a common underlying theme. An insight into one dream may unravel a whole series of dreams.*

- *Something that seems trivial or superficial in a dream may actually be masking a deep insight.*
- *Similarly, it is important for the analyst to pay attention to all the client's remarks, however trivial they may seem on the surface.*

However, Freud also warns that dream interpretation is not always easy. The elements of a dream can be interpreted in various ways and it is often doubtful which method to use in deciphering a given element:

- *Some elements can be taken in a positive or a negative sense – by this Freud seems to mean that a dream image may actually indicate its own opposite, for example hot/cold, fire/water and so on.*
- *An element may be interpreted historically – it is a recollection of something that has actually happened to the dreamer.*
- *The interpretation is sometimes to do with the wording – in other words, the element may contain a pun or other wordplay; for example, you might dream of a rather undesirable acquaintance who is wearing a pair of sunglasses that bear the trade name 'Wide Boy'.*
- *Some elements can be interpreted symbolically.*

Freudian symbols

Freud believed that much of a dream's content was disguised by means of symbols. Freudian symbols within dreams have become one of the most well-known aspects of psychoanalytic thinking. Freud believed that symbols had fixed meanings common to all humans, and therefore under certain circumstances it was possible to interpret a dream without actually questioning the dreamer, provided one knew a little about his personality, the circumstances of his life and the impressions that preceded the occurrence of the dream. However, symbols often have more than one meaning, so correct interpretation can only be arrived at by analysing the dream. To understand symbols in a dream Freud used a combination of two methods:

▶ *exploration of the dreamer's own associations*
▶ *using the analyst's knowledge of common dream symbols to fill in the gaps.*

Freud's own ideas about what dream symbols mean are notoriously sexual. So, for example:

▶ *Sticks, knives, umbrellas, trees and other pointy or penetrating objects represent the penis. So do objects from which water flows, such as taps, watering cans and fountains. For the male genitalia as a whole, the number 3 is of symbolic significance, whereas erections are symbolized by anything that rises into the air such as hot-air balloons and airships. It gets even odder – not only snakes, but also certain reptiles and fishes apparently represent penises, as do hats, overcoats and cloaks. Even Freud admits that the last three examples are hard to understand, but he declares that the symbolic connection is unquestionable.*
▶ *Boxes, chests and other containers represent the female genitalia. So do doors, gates and ships apparently, whereas cupboards, stoves and more especially rooms have more connection with the uterus. You can't escape from it – materials like wood and paper are symbols for women, as are tables, books ... no wonder Freud thought all dreams were sexual! Snails and mussels, however, do make a bit more sense as symbolizing the female genitalia.*
▶ *Sexual intercourse is symbolized by rhythmic activities such as dancing and riding, as well as things like climbing a ladder, or even going upstairs or running inside a house.*
▶ *Playing with a little child represents masturbation. So do all kinds of playing in a dream, as well as sliding, slipping or pulling branches off a tree.*

In this way, the dreaming mind uses symbols to conceal sexual thoughts and get past the censor. Freud certainly viewed symbols as being mainly used for purposes of concealment; however, he did warn that it was not always easy or straightforward to find an interpretation of a dream symbol. Not all of Freud's dream symbols are sexual. Falling into water or being raised out of it symbolizes birth; queens and kings represent parents; and so on. Freud said that we can learn the meanings of common symbols from various sources, such as myths and fairy tales, jokes, folklore, customs, sayings and songs. But he stuck firmly to his sexual theory and maintained that although symbolism in these and other fields, such as art and religion, was not always sexual, symbols in dreams were used almost exclusively for the expression of sexual objects and relations.

Origins of dreams

Freud noticed that a good deal of dream content came from recent events or emotional reactions. He explained that often these were actually distortions, masking deeper emotional issues that were connected to the recent events by long trains of association. In the same way, he maintained that childhood memories were also linked to recent events by associations. Thus, the latent content of the dream is often not really about current affairs at all. However, some part of the dream is always linked to a recent event – usually within 24 hours before the dream occurs. Sometimes these links are only revealed by a long process of free association.

Dreams frequently appear to be about trivial things: a recent event in the dreamer's life is directly represented in the dream. This kind of dream is often a wish-fulfilment dream, like the one Freud's own small daughter had about strawberries. Dreams of this sort are obviously straightforward and need little analysis, but Freud maintained that all dreams are significant because of their latent content. So, although the significance of some dreams is immediately obvious in this way, others need to be unravelled further by analysis before their real importance can be appreciated.

Sometimes, several recent events are blended together in the dream, in what Freud called condensation. This kind of dream often reveals deeper underlying issues when it is analysed. When displacement occurs, one or more recent events are represented in the dream but this time under the disguise of a more neutral recent event. This type of dream needs more thorough analysis to uncover the latent meaning. Sometimes an even more elaborate displacement occurs, where a deeply buried issue is disguised in the dream by an image of a more neutral recent event.

Modern psychologists have had a tendency, until recently, to see dreams merely as a kind of information processing – perhaps assimilating ideas about what has happened in waking life and then incorporating this information into memory banks. But dreams can certainly help us to solve ongoing problems, so there was a lot of truth in Freud's ideas. Recent research has suggested that the areas of the brain which control emotion and motivation are frequently aroused during REM (rapid eye movement) sleep – the phase of sleep when most dreaming occurs – so maybe Freud was not far off the mark. Dreams, as many writers will agree, also unleash creative processes – so the unconscious is not all about repressed and negative impulses as Freud tended to insist. However, the important thing is to recognize that it was Freud who played the biggest part in starting the process that led to the evolution of modern theories about the dreaming mind. For him the dream is all-important, 'one of the really deep and formative experiences of our soul', and so it forms one of the cornerstones of the psychoanalytic process.

THINGS TO REMEMBER

▶ *Dreams are of central importance in psychoanalysis.*

▶ *Freud saw dreams as wish fulfilments.*

▶ *He said that each dream has both a manifest and a latent content.*

▶ *He identified special mechanisms that prevented the latent content from becoming conscious.*

▶ *Freud believed that much of a dream's content was disguised by means of symbols.*

▶ *Freud interpreted dreams mainly in two ways – the symbolic method, which explores symbolic meaning and the decoding method, which uses traditional interpretations.*

▶ *He maintained that most dreams harked back to childhood experiences, particularly sexual ones.*

5

Exploring the unconscious

In this chapter you will learn:
* *Freud's theories about the structure and functioning of the mind*
* *about 'parapraxis' – the famous Freudian slip*
* *Freud's ideas about jokes and the unconscious.*

The divisions of the mind

Freud gradually became interested in extending his psychoanalytic exploration to try and discover how the 'normal' human mind operated. This step was important because it meant that psychoanalysis was no longer limited to psychology of the 'abnormal'. Freud's belief that the unconscious plays a huge part in determining the behaviour of 'normal' people means that his ideas have become important to ordinary people as well as psychiatrists and analysts, and that Freud himself has become more widely known as a result.

Psychoanalysis is all about bringing repressed ideas into consciousness, and Freud suggested that attacks against his ideas reflected this process in a collective sense, because people were trying to repress ideas that threatened current thinking. He said that the human race had had three huge blows to its self-esteem: the first was the realization that the earth revolves around the sun and not the other way around; the second was Darwin's theory of evolution; and the third was the discovery that it is the unconscious, and not the conscious mind, which rules our emotional life and hence, ultimately, our relationship to everything. Obviously he was secure in his belief that his own ideas were of paramount importance to the human race – he was in fact acting out the hero's life that he had dreamed of as a boy and which his mother had foretold for him from the moment of his birth.

In accordance with his insistence upon scientific thinking, Freud grappled with trying to formulate a theory about the structure of the mind. This was obviously difficult to achieve – one cannot trap the mind under a microscope or measure it in the laboratory – and he revised his ideas at various points throughout his life. One of the main difficulties was that, although he believed that the brain was the organ that controlled human consciousness, he realized that the divisions of the mind which he described could not be actual physical divisions of this organ. They really just gave a descriptive model to try and help us towards a better understanding of what was going on in the psyche.

To begin with, Freud decided that there were two states of consciousness:

▶ *The conscious mind is the part of the mind that is aware of its thoughts and actions. This is where all conscious thought processes occur – it is the source of conscious thinking, ideas and understanding. It is concerned with logical thinking, reality and civilized behaviour.*
▶ *The unconscious is seen as the part of the mind that is repressed, the place where we put all the stuff that our conditioning does not allow us to look at. Information in the unconscious cannot easily be dug out. A lot of our past history lies here too, some of which can only be recalled under hypnosis.*

After a while, Freud decided that this simple division was not quite right. He then proposed the existence of a third level:

▶ *The preconscious is the region of the mind between the conscious and the unconscious, where information is stored that is not conscious at the moment, but can easily be recalled when needed.*

If one imagines the psyche as a house, then the conscious mind could be the living quarters, and the **preconscious** a filing cabinet where information is stored ready for reference. The unconscious could be the cellar, or perhaps a loft, where stuff is stowed away and you need to use a ladder or dimly lit stairs to gain access.

Later on, Freud thought up a more complex model of the mind, based on these early ideas, where he suggests that the mind is composed of three parts – the **id**, the **ego** and the **super-ego**. This model will be discussed later in the book.

The theory of the unconscious

Freud saw the unconscious as being the part of the mind that lies outside the boundaries of consciousness. It was constructed by repression of ideas that were too painful or dangerous to be allowed to remain in the conscious mind, and also by **sublimation** – the re-channelling of instinctive drives for which an acceptable outlet cannot be found. These two processes were governed by laws of transformation. Freud saw the primary content of the unconscious as being sexual in nature, formed from sexual desires and urges that have been repressed.

Primitive instinctive urges had to be repressed and pushed down
into the unconscious in order for human society to function
properly, otherwise everyone would just act on impulse all the
time and there could be no rules or structure. Each child had to
go through a series of developmental stages where this repression
of instincts was gradually accomplished – for example they had
to be potty trained, learn not to hit other children and so on.
Freud believed that the sex drive in particular was so strong that
it constantly threatened to force its way up to the surface and
take over, but he did not think it was the only drive that governs
human behaviour. In his later writing he suggested that there were
a huge number of instincts, or drives, in the psyche, which can
all be grouped into two main categories: **Eros** (the life instinct)
and **Thanatos** (the death instinct). Urges linked to Thanatos were
destructive and therefore worked against the sex drive, which is
obviously basically creative in its nature.

Insight
> Thanatos: Freud actually used the word 'Todestrieb',
> meaning death drive. He describes it in *Beyond the Pleasure
> Principle* as 'an urge inherent in all organic life to restore
> an earlier state of things'. Eros on the other hand, is the
> life instinct, which is concerned with self-preservation and
> enjoyment and so encourages love and creativity.

Freud's fascination with ancient history emerged again in his ideas
about the unconscious when he suggested that the developmental
process in the individual child also reflected the entire history of

the human race. So, each individual has their own private life history, which emerges during dream work and analysis, but there is also a bigger picture, common to all of us, which manifests as built-in symbolic connections that the individual has not acquired by learning. It was this idea that later inspired the psychologist C. G. Jung, and led him to develop his theory of the Collective Unconscious.

In 1915, Freud wrote a paper called 'The Unconscious', which explains why he thinks his theory of the unconscious is the best way of understanding what really governs our behaviour. The existence of the unconscious sheds light upon puzzling aspects of our mental world, such as ideas that 'spring from nowhere', strange inexplicable urges, and dreams.

Unconscious mental states are similar to conscious ones – people can have unconscious beliefs, emotions, desires, thoughts and so on. Freud soon realized that not everything in the unconscious is repressed material: some of it is just stuff that happens not to be conscious at the moment. This is why he initially decided that there had to be a third area – the preconscious – containing information that we are not thinking about at a given moment, but which is easily accessible when we need it. An example of this could be a foreign language that we were taught at school but have not really used since.

On the other hand, suppressed material in the unconscious is blocked and therefore cannot be accessed directly. It can, however, be accessed through studying dreams and parapraxes (slips of the tongue). Freud discusses these ideas in his book *Psychopathology of Everyday Life*. Another way of accessing the unconscious is through jokes, which Freud believes are always an expression of repressed wishes. He discusses this idea in *Jokes and their Relation to the Unconscious*.

Some of these ideas seem like pseudo-science to the modern mind, but it is important to remember that the concept of the unconscious is of vital importance to modern psychoanalytical theory, as well as to other areas of study such as the study of dreams. For example, it was through Freud's ideas that we began to realize that our dreams are meaningful and that they arise partly in order to help us deal with problems that are not being sorted out by our conscious minds. The idea of the unconscious is now so built-in to our cultural thinking that it is very hard for us to imagine what a huge impact Freud's new way of thinking had on society at the time.

The pleasure principle and the reality principle

Freud suggested two opposing processes that control normal human behaviour.

▶ *The pleasure principle pushes people towards immediate gratification of their wishes. This is the tendency behind all natural impulses and basic urges. It is linked to the unconscious and it is impulsive, primitive and disorganized. According to Freud, it rules people right from birth and is basically to do with the gratification of sexual urges. At first Freud did not seem to consider other drives, such as hunger, when he was talking about the pleasure principle. Later, he effectively redefined the concept of 'sexuality' to encompass any form of pleasure to do with bodily functions. According to Freud, the pleasure principle is always the main motive force of the unconscious.*
▶ *As a person matures and has to operate in a social environment, the opposing force, the reality principle, comes into play. It involves conscious, logical thinking, and it allows us to delay gratification in order to get on with everyday life. For example, although the sex drive is so strong, people gradually discover as they grow up that it is not always acceptable or practical to indulge sexual urges at the time and place that they arise.*

Freud said there were two main types of mental functioning – 'primary process', which is governed by wish fulfilment and the pleasure principle; and 'secondary process', which is governed by conscious thought and the reality principle. Neurotic people found reality unbearable and so they escaped from it by means of fantasies and daydreams developing out of children's play. In adult life, these were split off and kept free from reality testing, so that they were only governed by the pleasure principle.

Freud used the word **libido** to describe the sexual drive, which he claimed was the driving force for most behaviour. The reality principle causes libidinal (sexual) energy to be redirected into safer or more socially acceptable behaviour, for example some kind of creative work. This unconscious redirection is called sublimation.

Insight

In Freud's thinking libido is mainly a sexual drive, as it tends to be in modern common usage. Others, notably Carl Jung, have seen it more as a general, creative psychic energy.

According to Freud, psychological problems arise as a result of the conflict between sexual drive (ruled by the pleasure principle) and survival (ruled by the reality principle). After a while, however, he changed his mind about the two forces being in opposition. He decided that they actually worked together, because in the long run both led to a decrease in tension. This decrease in tension was held to be the purpose of all behaviour.

Freud was often criticized for modifying his ideas in this way. He found this criticism annoying and pointed out that by changing their views people are often seen as fickle and unreliable, yet by not changing their views they are seen as obstinate and pig-headed. He said it was very tiresome to be criticized for holding views that had been modified long ago.

It seems typical of Freud's earnest outlook on life that the pleasure principle is really all about avoiding pain, rather than about pleasures such as love, joy, fun and friendship! Freud always tended to view any powerful emotion as negative – something that needed to be expelled in order for a person to feel comfortable. According to Freud, a person's character is determined by the way libido is channelled into more acceptable activity. If libido is blocked up without an outlet, then neuroses or other psychological problems develop. Psychoanalysis is all about finding out what urges have been blocked up and why.

BEYOND THE PLEASURE PRINCIPLE

As usual, Freud tried to stick to a scientific approach in his thinking, following the idea current at the time in biology that living organisms always strive to achieve stability and equilibrium. But during his clinical work with patients, he gradually found that there were times when his theory that pleasure is always produced by a simple relief of tension was not adequate.

In fact there were various flaws in the idea of the pleasure principle. Firstly, Freud observed that in normal sexual behaviour there is often a tendency to put off the final orgasm for as long as possible. He observed a similar thing happening in small children, who would hold back a bowel movement, apparently because it gave them some kind of satisfaction to do this. If relief of tension were the only goal, then why should people put off that goal? Freud came to the conclusion that this behaviour simply prolonged the actual pleasure on the way to the ultimate climax. This was what he called foreplay.

Harder to explain was the fact that Freud found that patients who suffered from neuroses caused by trauma tended to keep on endlessly acting out the original scene in their imagination. Small children also do this in a more concrete way, by repeatedly acting out nasty experiences. This probably gives them some sense of control over the original incident. Freud noticed that horrific scenes of real-life experiences tended to surface endlessly in the dreams of traumatized adults, without any apparent disguise or distortion. Such dreams were sometimes so awful that the sufferers were frightened to go to sleep at all, which meant that the dream was apparently failing in its main function – that of safeguarding sleep.

Freud slowly began to evolve new theories as an attempt to deal with this problem, involving other instinctive drives such as aggression. But it was not until 1920 that he published a paper called 'Beyond the Pleasure Principle', which discussed some of these ideas. He suggested that people could sometimes develop a repetition compulsion, endlessly repeating the same scene – some of his patients obsessively relived the same childhood scenes over and over again without ever achieving any progress. Sometimes this kind of repetitive behaviour fits in with the idea of the pleasure principle – anybody who deals with young children and has to read the same story over and over again will see this in action! But sometimes the repetition is obviously not pleasurable at all and actually causes the person to suffer. This eventually led Freud to develop the idea of Thanatos, the death instinct (see Chapter 8).

Parapraxis, the famous Freudian slip

Parapraxis is a general term for the now famous Freudian slip. The plural is parapraxes, and the word is derived from Greek words meaning 'alongside normal practice'. Freud never actually used the term himself – he used the word *Fehlleistung*, or 'faulty achievement', meaning a slip that happens when we intend to say or do one thing and actually end up saying or doing another. He listed various categories of mistakes of this sort, such as slips of the tongue, forgetting proper names, mistakes in reading and writing and so on. Parapraxis is now used as a convenient blanket term to cover all of these, and in psychoanalysis a slip of this kind implies that unconscious wishes are being expressed.

Freud became interested in parapraxes because they occurred frequently in the lives of perfectly 'normal' people, and seemed to him to demonstrate that the unconscious was at work. His popular book, *The Psychopathology of Everyday Life*, is all about parapraxes. The title of the book is interesting in itself, because his choice of the word psychopathology – the study of abnormal mental processes – implies that Freud believed parapraxes to be symptoms of abnormality or disorder, despite their universal occurrence.

Freud identified a whole list of different forms of parapraxis. For example:

- *forgetting people's names*
- *forgetting something one intended to do*
- *slips of the tongue or pen*
- *misreading or mishearing*
- *losing or temporarily mislaying things*
- *bungled actions and accidents*
- *remembering things wrongly.*

Freud said that none of these are actually innocent accidental mistakes. Like all mental phenomena in Freud's view, they have a clearly definable cause. They all reveal the unconscious at work on a cover-up job again, rather like the dreaming process. Thoughts that have been repressed because they are painful or socially unacceptable are disguised by means of a Freudian slip. The slip is seen not as a silly chance mistake but as an unconscious mental act.

Slips of speech are often caused by the influence of something that is connected to the misspoken word by a chain of thought. Sometimes they occur when the person anticipates a taboo word coming up, or perhaps feels that the conversation is getting uncomfortably close to revealing his or her true feelings.

In fact, any kind of parapraxis arises as a result of two different intentions in a person's mind that are acting in opposition. If they are analysed it can be seen that they reveal what the person is *really* thinking. According to Freud, all parapraxes occur in this way, although it is not possible actually to *prove* that his theory is true. Other psychologists argued that parapraxes are caused by factors such as fatigue, excitement or distraction. Freud admitted that this was true, but insisted that it missed the point – such conditions simply make it easier or more likely for slips to occur.

Freud could be very clever and persuasive when he wanted to argue a point, but he sometimes carried this too far: some of the examples of parapraxis that he gives in *The Psychopathology of Everyday Life* seem very contrived and convoluted. In some cases it is difficult to grasp how the unconscious mind could possibly have gone through such a lengthy process in the split second it took to produce the original slip of the tongue!

However, other examples that he gives in the book are much more succinct and amusing, and we can all relate to them, so it certainly seems that Freud had hit upon something in his theory. For example, there is the case of the American man living in Europe who almost wrote to his wife suggesting that she come to visit him, sailing on the *Lusitania*, as he had done himself. This would have been a mistake: the *Lusitania* had already been sunk by a German submarine during the First World War. The man had actually travelled to Europe on a ship called the *Mauretania*. Some more examples of parapraxis are given below.

FORGETTING PROPER NAMES

Freud gives an example where, try as he might, he could not recall a place name. In the end he had to ask his womenfolk for help. They were amused, saying that of course he would forget a name like that – the place was called Nervi. They were laughing at the idea that Freud had so much to do with nerves in his daily work that he had pushed the name out of his mind. Very often a wrong proper name will intrude in speech in place of the correct one. When this occurs the two are usually connected by a train of associations. The subconscious wants to forget the correct name because it has painful or embarrassing associations, or it may just be connected with a topic one has had enough of – such as the work example given by Freud.

Parapraxis in action.

Interestingly, Freud points out that forgetting names is very contagious – if one person has difficulty recalling a name it is common for a friend to struggle too.

FORGETTING CHILDHOOD MEMORIES

Many childhood memories are not consciously recalled by the adult. Freud observed that children frequently remember trivial events rather than important ones. He seems to overlook the possibility that sometimes children might seem to remember trivia because for them those are the very things that have assumed importance. Instead, he says that a process of displacement is going on – the child substitutes a trivial memory in order to conceal a painful one. Freud calls this type of memory a concealing memory, and says that they form a large part of our total memory bank. Some people can remember events from as far back as six months of age, but others cannot remember a thing before they were about eight. Freud says that this is particularly interesting because children of four are capable of quite complicated thinking and emotions, so it seems likely that some sort of blocking mechanism is at work, which reinforces his theory that neuroses have their origin in early childhood.

Freud says that it is very difficult to give examples of this type of concealing memory, even though they commonly crop up during psychoanalysis. This is mainly because in order to unravel the concealing memory you would have to understand the person's whole life history. One example he did provide, however, was from a man who recalled a scene from when he was five years old. He was having difficulty distinguishing the letter n from the letter m, and begged his aunt to explain. The aunt explained that the m had 'one whole portion more'. This memory apparently concealed the fact that he was also exploring the difference between boys and girls, and would dearly have liked this particular aunt to explain to him that a boy also had 'one portion more than the girl'.

ACCIDENTS

Even accidents such as tripping over are parapraxes. Freud says that they show unconscious feelings being expressed in a physical way. We all know examples of people who seem to get themselves injured almost on purpose in order to be able to lap up attention. Conversely, we sometimes 'accidentally' hurt another person when we feel hostile towards them, or we may break an object such as a hideous vase because of a subconscious desire to get rid of it.

Freud gives various examples of bungled actions. For example, Freud forbade one of his patients to contact a girl with whom he was madly in love. The patient accidentally asked directory enquiries for her telephone number when he was actually trying to contact Freud. This shows that bungled actions, like other errors, are often used to fulfil wishes that a person is consciously trying to deny.

SLIPS OF THE TONGUE

These are very common and one can easily observe amusing ones in everyday conversation. Freud gives lots of examples of the common Malapropism, where sound confusion errors occur, such as the man who 'entrusted his money to a savings crank'. Another example is the rather hard-up patient who begged him not to prescribe her 'big bills', because she couldn't swallow them. This category also includes Spoonerisms, where parts of words are displaced, such as in 'the student had tasted the whole worm'. The slip of the tongue can often be seen to be transparently covering up what the person would really like to have said.

FORGETTING FOREIGN WORDS

Freud said that we are less likely to forget completely a word in our native tongue than in a foreign language – a slip is more likely to appear instead. He goes on at great length about an occasion when he was trying to remember the name of an artist called Signorelli. He kept getting Botticelli or Boltraffio in his mind instead. His explanation for this covers about six pages in *Psychopathology of Everyday Life*, and involves a complicated diagram with such labels as 'death and sexuality' and 'repressed thoughts'. It is all very interesting and ingenious, but somehow the arrangement seems rather unlikely. Is the unconscious really that desperate to conceal fairly trivial thoughts? And how does it work out such a complex series of connections so quickly? The problem with this type of analysis is that it relies mainly on the free-association technique. This method usually leads quite rapidly to the uncovering of supposedly significant, emotionally charged material, even if you start with an innocent, neutral word: but this doesn't really prove that what has emerged was the original cause of the parapraxis.

SLIPS OF THE PEN

Slips of the pen, like slips of the tongue, are common and easily recorded. Freud tells of an incident when he came home from holiday in September, and on starting work wrote the date as October 20th. The explanation was that he was experiencing a lull in his work after the holiday period and had a client booked in to see him on the October date, so the slip was a kind of wish-fulfilment process, wishing that the date would hurry up and arrive.

Often, slips of the pen show up our hidden intentions towards the person to whom we are writing. Freud gives the example of a woman who wrote a friendly letter to her sister congratulating her on her new home, but when she came to address the envelope she wrote an old address – that of a cramped apartment that her sister had lived in long before. When a friend pointed out this 'error' to her, she sadly admitted that she was indeed jealous and begrudged her sister's good fortune.

ERRONEOUS ACTIONS

Freud says that since slips of the tongue are motor functions, we would expect to find similar lapses in other actions. He gives an example of this: when he used to visit the homes of his patients he would sometimes find that instead of knocking on the door or ringing the bell he would pull his own key out of his pocket and then stand there feeling rather silly. When he analysed these occurrences he discovered that they only occurred when he was visiting houses where he felt 'at home'. Freud cites other examples of people telling him that they tried to open the door to their office with their own house keys. Losing one's keys or using the wrong key is often a symbolic pointer to where we would rather be.

Erroneous actions may sometimes be advantageous. Freud gives an example of this too, describing an incident involving a cane with a silver handle that he had once owned. Through no fault of his own, the thin silver plate was damaged and he had the cane repaired, but this was not done in a very satisfactory way. Later on, while romping with his children, he used the cane to hook one of their legs – the cane was broken in the process and this allowed him to get rid of it without feeling guilty.

Jokes and the unconscious

Freud was also interested in the way jokes demonstrate the workings of the unconscious. His book *Jokes and Their Relation to the Unconscious*, which appeared in 1905, is quite a collection of mainly Jewish jokes. Unfortunately, there are cultural and language problems in translation so that many of the jokes do not come across very well in English. The main point he made was that jokes are another indication of the repression and sublimation of unconscious material. This may either be the work of an internal censor mechanism, or it may be due to the presence of another person who might be shocked. In the second case, when the shocking idea is presented under disguise in the form of a joke, it is still done in order to evade internal inhibitions in the mind of the person telling the joke. So, the joke is really a way of expressing something that is normally banned by society. The pleasure gained by telling a joke in this way gives a sudden release of pent-up energy.

Some of the mechanisms used in jokes are the same as those used in dreams, for example one word is substituted for another, or condensation is used. Freud identified various mechanisms at work in jokes:

▶ Condensation – *a composite word is formed, or a word is modified.*
▶ Repetition – *the same material is used in various different ways during the joke.*
▶ Double meaning – *jokes which play upon words and one thing is used to represent another.*

Freud identified two categories of joke:

▶ **Tendentious jokes** – *this type is dependent on indirect expression of hostility or sexual urges. The category would include classic mother-in-law jokes, and dirty jokes.*
▶ **Innocent jokes** – *these depend on verbal ingenuity. The category would include puns and riddles.*

The first category is the one in which Freud was chiefly interested. These are the jokes that allow the joker to get around internal inhibition by expressing a sexual or aggressive urge indirectly, as in schoolboy humour, where rude jokes are told to relieve adolescent tension. Freud eventually claimed that *all* jokes are in fact tendentious, even the innocent ones that play with words, which he saw as a kind of mental foreplay, leading up to the tendentious ones! This was a rather circular argument really – any pleasure derived from clever wordplay must be a minor form of pleasure, because the only real pleasure had to be derived from the release of sexual tension.

Even jokes that allowed a person to express aggression fitted this rule, because at this stage of his thinking Freud still saw aggression merely as a sadistic aspect of the sexual instinct. It is a dismal fact that Freud tended to reduce everything to the need to release libidinal tension. Why overlook fun, clever wordplay, or the cathartic effect of simply having a good laugh among friends?

Much of Freud's work that we have covered in this chapter – dreams, the pleasure and reality principles, parapraxes and jokes – is actually looking at ways in which the ego defends itself. If the ego finds an idea too painful, embarrassing or socially unacceptable, the idea is repressed. The unconscious then finds endless little ways of letting the ideas leak back out.

THINGS TO REMEMBER

▶ *Freud originally divided the mind into three sections – the conscious, preconscious and unconscious.*

▶ *Freud said that the unconscious was formed by repression of ideas that were too painful to keep in the conscious mind.*

▶ *Sublimation is the process of re-channelling unacceptable instinctive drives.*

▶ *Freud suggested two opposing processes that controlled human behaviour. These were the pleasure principle and the reality principle.*

▶ *Psychic conflicts arise as a result of conflict between the two processes.*

▶ *Freud was interested in parapraxes (Freudian slips) and jokes because they showed the unconscious mind at work in 'normal' people.*

6

....

Sexual theories

In this chapter you will learn:

- *how Freud's new theories about sex caused uproar in the scientific community*
- *Freud's theories about sexual deviations*
- *theories about infantile sexuality and how sexuality develops.*

Freud attacks current thinking

Theories about sexuality and sexual development became important in psychoanalysis from an early stage. Freud published his book *Three Essays on the Theory of Sexuality* in 1905. Alongside his earlier book, *The Interpretation of Dreams*, this was to be one of his most important works because it outlines the foundation for his theory of neurosis, explaining why people need to repress things and what unconscious, instinctive drives affect their behaviour. The three essays in the book cover three main areas of his thinking about sexuality: sexual deviations or aberrations, infantile sexuality, and developments that occur at puberty.

This seems a strange order in which to write the book, but of course Freud was dealing mostly with adults in his medical practice, so logically this would have been the starting point for his thought process. As a result of his work with neurotic adults,

Freud began to ask himself whether sexual aberrations arose from some innate disposition, or were acquired later as a result of experiences in life. Later on he himself decided to introduce his readers to the subject of sexuality by discussing infantile sexuality first.

Typically, Freud constantly developed and modified his ideas, so the *Three Essays on the Theory of Sexuality* were revised many times over the 20 years following publication. He explained that it was very difficult to define exactly what was meant by the word 'sexual', and that most people had a very limited concept of what the word meant. To say that it meant everything to do with the differences between the two sexes was too vague. On the other hand, the view that it was only concerned with actual genital contact between two people of the opposite sex was too limiting. This view would mean that sex was only connected with what Freud saw as being 'improper'. There again, to say that it just referred to everything to do with reproduction would leave out obviously sexual things such as kissing and masturbation.

Freud concluded that the word sexual concerned all these things and more. He then went on to write various additional letters and papers connected with sexuality during his life, which covered a broad spectrum, including topics such as the sexual theories of children, the taboo of virginity, fetishism and female sexuality.

Freud knew that the ideas he was presenting in his new book about sexuality would meet with enormous resistance. The accepted view at the time was that sex was all about efforts to bring the genitals into contact with those of somebody of the opposite sex.

This naturally also involved kissing, looking at and touching the other person, but the behaviour was only concerned with reproduction. Infantile sexuality was seen as being totally dormant and sexual behaviour did not appear until puberty, when the body became sexually mature. Before this it was only brought out into the open accidentally when the child was sexually abused by an adult; experiences of this sort led to neurotic disturbances later in the person's life. Initially, Freud thought this too, but by 1897 he had abandoned this 'seduction theory', and decided that children have sexual impulses right from the beginning and don't need any outside influence to trigger them.

As he had expected, Freud caused uproar when he suggested that people needed to take a much broader view in order to study sex scientifically. He pointed out that:

▶ *Homosexual people are often only attracted sexually to members of their own sex. They may even find the opposite sex repellent. Freud called this group of people 'inverts'. For them, sexuality has nothing to do with the reproductive process.*
▶ *For other people the sexual drive disregards the genitals or their normal use. They may be turned on by inappropriate body parts, inanimate objects, and so on. Freud said that the words 'sexual' and 'genital' therefore had very different meanings. Freud calls this group of people 'perverts'.*
▶ *Psychoanalytical research had shown that neurotic problems and perversions were often caused by early childhood sexual experiences. As children were not supposed to have a sex life, this suggestion caused particular furore.*

Freud's theories about sexuality were so new and challenging that even by the time he wrote a preface to the fourth edition of *Three Essays on the Theory of Sexuality* in 1920 he was still defending his position. By then people had accepted many of his other ideas, but his sexual theories were still being ridiculed and some people were challenging the whole psychoanalytical theory because they claimed that it said absolutely everything could be explained by sex.

Freud tried to give academic backing to his ideas by suggesting that they had parallels in the work of Schopenhauer and Plato, both famous philosophers. He suggested that people often rejected sexual theories because they felt threatened by them and so they wanted to block them out – thus once more rather cunningly 'proving' the validity of his own ideas. He also pointed out that early childhood sexuality could only be investigated by somebody such as a psychoanalyst, who had a great deal of time to devote to the process. In many cases there simply was not enough time or money to do this and so the very early childhood experiences would never be unearthed.

What Freud was really doing was extending the concept of what was sexual, emphasizing that sexuality was important in all human achievements, not just in the reproduction of the species. He did this in order to support his theory that neuroses were caused by sexual problems and that neurotic symptoms therefore had sexual meaning. He found that neurotics often showed great resistance to any mention of sex, and that their sexual urges were often very strongly repressed. 'Normal' people, on the other hand, satisfied their sexual urges in ordinary sexual activity and in dreams.

Sexual deviations

From his work with neurotic patients, Freud came to the conclusion that tendencies to all kinds of sexual deviation existed unconsciously in many people and led to the formation of neurotic symptoms. In fact, he went so far as to suggest that initial tendencies to 'perversion' are universal in the sense that the sexual urges of the infant are not aimed at a specific object. 'Normal' sexual behaviour, that is behaviour which is aimed specifically at an adult member of the opposite sex, develops gradually as a result of inhibitions that occur during maturation.

The inhibitions that gradually lead the growing child towards 'normal' sexual behaviour arise as a result of reactions from other people (such as shock or disgust) when the child displays unacceptable sexual behaviour. The moral structure imposed by society as a whole is also very important. When this process goes wrong or gets stuck in some way, then sexual deviations become apparent. Freud defines various types of sexual deviation, which he divides into two groups:

▶ *Deviations in respect of the* **sexual object** – *the sexual object is the person or thing from which the sexual attraction comes.*
▶ *Deviations in respect of the* **sexual aim** – *the sexual aim is the sexual act that a person is driven towards.*

This division seems fairly artificial and even Freud seems to get rather muddled about it at times, for example, he says that fetishism could go into either category.

Insight

Freud's distinction between the sexual object and the sexual aim is perhaps another example of his trying to be precise and scientific, when actually the human psyche is not always quite so easy to analyse.

INVERSION

This is the word Freud uses for homosexuality: the word implies an in-turning of the libido onto an object like oneself. In other words, the sexual object is never fully separate from the self. This way of thinking partly goes back to early childhood when the child does not recognize sex differences and is very close to the mother, who supplies all its needs regardless of its sex. Freud saw all sexual deviations in this way – as examples of an incomplete maturity of sexual object or aim.

Freud recognizes different types of behaviour in this category:

▶ *some people go exclusively for their own sex*
▶ *some are happy with either sex*
▶ *some people turn to their own sex when the need arises, e.g. in prison.*

Freud goes on to say that some inverts accept their sexuality as a natural state of affairs, whereas others are horrified by it and see it as a pathological compulsion. In the more extreme cases the person has been an invert from a very early age and is more likely to have accepted the state of affairs.

Freud was not able to identify one single sexual aim among inverts, nor was it possible to find a satisfactory explanation for the origin of inversion. But he did say that it points us to one important fact – that the sexual instinct does not always draw everybody to the same object. In fact, it is surprisingly common for deviations to occur.

ORAL AND ANAL SEX

Oral and anal sex were definitely considered as perversions by Freud. He said that a feeling of disgust prevents most people from indulging in either perversion. This sense of disgust is one of the natural repressive mechanisms that make people develop in the direction of normal sexuality. However, this feeling can go too far, so that the genitals of the opposite sex seem totally disgusting too. Freud found this to be a common reaction among hysterics.

Freud says that in early childhood sexual excitation arises as a kind of by-product of normal processes that occur in the body. There are various **erotogenic zones** in the body: areas where certain stimuli, especially rubbing, produce feelings of pleasure.

Insight

An erotogenic zone is the same thing as an erogenous zone, or an erotogenous zone. People love to invent posh, scientific-sounding words, especially for subjects that are slightly taboo.

Examples are the mouth, the anus and the genitalia, each of which exert their own influence on the child as it goes through a series of maturational changes. At this early stage, the sexual instinct is not focused on a specific external object but is auto-erotic, i.e. the child is turned on by parts of itself. As sucking is one of the first things from which the infant gets satisfaction, oral sex obviously relates back to a very early stage. Similarly, anal sex is linked back to a child's first awareness of the pleasure to be gained from emptying the bowels.

FETISHISM

Fetishism occurs when the normal sexual object becomes replaced by an object that bears some relation to it. The fetish object is usually something normally considered to be non-sexual, for example a different part of the body such as the hair or the feet. In other cases it is an inanimate object, such as an item of clothing. Freud said that fetishism usually occurred as the result of a sexual experience in early childhood. A symbolic train of thought later connects the fetish to the sexual urge.

Sometimes this train of thought is fairly easy to track – for example, fur may relate to pubic hair, and so on – but it is not always that straightforward. Freud was particularly interested in fetishism because it produced such a bizarre range of behaviours, but he said that to some extent it is present in all of us, especially if the normal sexual aim is unattainable. Freud gives us the rather innocent example of someone yearning over a handkerchief or a garter that has been close to the loved one. In extreme cases, however, the power of the fetish may be so great that it completely takes the place of any kind of human relationship. In this case it can be seen to reflect an incomplete development of both sexual object and sexual aim.

SEX WITH CHILDREN OR ANIMALS

Freud was quite tolerant of homosexual people, saying that they could be 'quite sound in other respects'. This sounds patronizing to us today, but considering the times in which he lived, when homosexuality was repressed by society, it is really quite a liberal point of view. However, he definitely frowned upon people who had sex with children, saying that they were too cowardly or impotent to find a more appropriate object. His attitude to sexual intercourse with animals (not uncommon amongst country people, where lack of availability of an appropriate sexual object could lead them to override the species barrier) was similar. Freud says that this kind of behaviour throws light on the sexual instinct, which permits huge variation and lack of discrimination in its objects: in fact, at times it seems almost any old thing will do. This does not happen with hunger – another basic biological drive – except in very extreme circumstances.

TOUCHING AND LOOKING

Tactile and visual stimulation between sexual partners only constituted a perversion to Freud if:

- *they were restricted only to the genitals*
- *they were involved with the overcoming of disgust, for example in voyeurism, or in people who enjoy watching excretory functions*
- *they totally supplanted the normal sexual aim, instead of just leading up to it.*

The opposite of voyeurism is exhibitionism, which is the urge to display the sexual organs and hopefully to see the other person's too – 'show me yours and I'll show you mine'. Both conditions often crop up in the same person. In small children there is obviously no shame in running around naked and happily showing off the body – this is perfectly normal – but as the child grows older, shame gradually arises and this is the force that normally opposes voyeurism and exhibitionism in adult life.

SADISM AND MASOCHISM

This is another pair of complementary opposites, and Freud saw them as being the most common and significant of the perversions. Sadism is the desire to inflict pain or humiliation on the sexual object, masochism is the opposite – the desire to receive pain or humiliation from the sexual object. Freud said that the roots of these two perversions are easy to detect. In the normal male, sexuality has a strong element of aggression – there is the desire to overcome resistance and dominate the sexual partner. In sadism this urge gets out of hand. (One could ask how this explanation accounts for sadistic behaviour in women.) Masochism seemed to Freud to be further removed from the normal sexual aim – he said that it was probably caused primarily through guilt and fear, and saw it as a kind of extension of sadism turned in upon the self.

Freud added that there was definitely a connection between cruelty and the sexual instinct in the history of human civilization, but he was not able to explain why – he suggested that a number of factors combined to produce this single result. He was particularly interested in his observation that sadism and masochism are habitually found together in the same person, although one aspect often dominates. He saw this contrast between activity and passivity as being one of the universal characteristics of sexual life, reflecting the basic opposing forces of masculinity and femininity.

Freud drew several conclusions from his study of sexual deviations:

▶ *The sexual instinct has to struggle against various mental resistances. This is probably a mechanism to keep the sexual instinct restrained within what is considered to be 'normal'.*
▶ *Some perversions are complex in their origin. This shows that the sexual instinct is much more complicated than people had previously maintained.*
▶ *The sexuality of neurotics has usually remained in, or been brought back to, an infantile state. This discovery brought Freud to the study of infantile sexuality.*

Infantile sexuality

The popular view in Freud's day was that sexuality lay dormant until puberty. Psychologists writing about child development generally omitted any reference to sexuality. This was probably mainly because it was 'not nice' to mention sex at all, so to imply that children thought about it was the ultimate horror. Once again,

Freud stuck his neck out and suggested two main reasons for the silence about infant sexuality:

▶ *the taboo aspect*
▶ *the fact that most people tend to forget what happens to them before the age of six or eight years.*

Freud thought that this second aspect was strange, because small children show plenty of evidence of awareness and insight into what is going on in their lives. However, early recollections could be brought to light under hypnosis. Freud therefore proposed that there was a special process of infantile **amnesia** (a process of forgetting that may be total or partial), that went into action to repress thoughts about sexual experiences.

So, according to Freud, sexual impulses are present from birth but are soon overcome by a progressive process of repression. This process comes about as the child discovers that it has to comply with various rules in order to fit into society. Feelings of disgust and shame begin to arise and these suppress the sexual urge. The process of infantile amnesia is the forerunner of and basis for the process of hysterical amnesia in adult life.

According to Freud, infantile sexuality is not concerned only with the genital region but shows up at different stages of development in various parts of the body, such as the oral zone, the anal zone and finally the genital zone. The aim of all infantile sexual activity is to get satisfaction by stimulating an erotogenic zone, but by the age of about six or eight years, this early sexual activity goes dormant until puberty. This is known as the **latency period**.

Insight

For more about the latency period, see Chapter 7.

INFANT EXPLORATION OF SEXUALITY

Children are naturally curious about sex. Freud says that they explore sexuality in various ways. Often, when a threatening younger sibling arrives, one of the first things the older child wants to know is where babies come from, but many of them are dissatisfied by nursery explanations such as the stork bringing them. Misunderstandings are common too, for example, children may think the baby is born through the anus, because they are used to the idea of faeces appearing in this way.

Small children are also curious to find out about the opposite sex. There was not so much scope for this in Freud's day because children were kept 'decently' covered up. The eventual revelation was often very traumatic according to Freud – for boys it led to a 'castration **complex**'.

Insight

We all have the odd complex lurking in our unconscious – they develop as a result of our unique life experiences and tend to be associated with a particular subject or theme. Our attitudes and behaviour are influenced by these personal complexes, but they are difficult to spot in oneself because of course they are unconscious. Things that one tends to get het up about are often powerful pointers to a hidden complex.

Having observed that little girls had no penis, the boy was terrified that he would somehow lose his own. This could lead to fantasies about the penis being damaged during sexual intercourse with a woman – hence the alarming idea of the 'vagina dentata', a ferocious vagina with teeth waiting to rip off the penis! Such fears could be one reason for some men preferring to stick to intercourse with their own sex.

Insight

One is tempted to speculate that Freud suffered from a castration complex as a child and so developed this as a theory that applied to all small boys.

For girls there was also a castration complex, because when they discovered that boys have a penis it was immediately obvious to them that they had somehow lost their own. This led to a terrible 'penis envy', where the little girl was overcome with jealousy at the marvellous male organ and immediately starting wanting to be a boy. This urge was sometimes replaced later by a desire to have a baby, which in some way could make up for the missing penis.

Freud also claimed that if a child witnessed adults having sex, it invariably thought that they were fighting, and glimpses of menstrual blood on sheets or underwear only served to confirm this horrid suspicion. Because children were not supposed to have sexual feelings at all, people generally concealed any information about sex from them until puberty, when, if they were lucky, they got a rudimentary explanation at best. To his great credit, Freud totally disagreed with all this secrecy. He argued that children are naturally curious about sexual matters, as they are about everything. Therefore, he suggested that questions about sex that arise at home should be answered truthfully from the outset, and that children should be properly educated about sex in school before the age of ten.

The struggles of puberty

Freud's ideas about what happened at puberty, explained in the third of the *Three Essays on the Theory of Sexuality*, gained far more acceptance at the time than his ideas about infant sexuality and sexual deviance. He said that sexual changes in the physical body begin to occur at puberty and change the whole pattern of infantile sexuality. The latency period ends and hormonal changes cause a huge resurgence of the powerful sexual drive which was present in infancy:

▶ *The child's first sexual feelings arise from sucking at the mother's breast. At this very early stage the mother is the sexual object.*
▶ *Next is the stage of infantile sexuality where the child is excited by the sensations in its own body. This stage is*

autoerotic – the infant derives pleasure from its own body, so the child's own body is the sexual object. Sexual activity at this stage is derived from a number of separate instinctive urges, such as eating, or emptying the bowels.

▶ *At puberty the child begins to be attracted to members of the opposite sex. A new sexual object, outside the self, now has to be discovered and all the component instincts of the sexual drive now have to combine to attain the new sexual aim.*

Freud maintains that a normal sexual life is only attained at puberty by the coming together of two currents of energy directed towards the sexual object and the sexual aim. At puberty, the two sexes diverge greatly because different functions emerge for their sexual aims. According to Freud, the development of sexual inhibitions of sexuality appears earlier in little girls, and in the face of less resistance. Rather bizarrely, he views the early autoerotic and masturbatory activity of the infant as being 'wholly masculine' in both sexes. In fact, he maintains that libido is invariably of a masculine nature, whether it occurs in men or women. In little girls the erotogenic zone is the clitoris, which is **homologous** (i.e. fundamentally similar in structure) to the penis.

At puberty, the sexual organs grow and become functional in the reproductive sense. Freud says that observations show that stimuli work on the complex sexual apparatus from three directions, namely the external world, the organic interior of the body, and mental activity. All three kinds of stimuli produce sexual excitement of two kinds: mental and physical. The mental excitement gives rise to a feeling of tension and the physical excitement gives rise to changes in the genitalia in preparation for the sexual act. Freud insists that although sexual arousal is undeniably pleasurable, the accompanying sexual tension necessarily involves 'unpleasure'. This fits in with his idea that the body is constantly seeking a state of equilibrium.

The development of the sexual organs at puberty causes new sexual tensions. Freud says that in boys there is a great increase in libido, which is fairly straightforward because the new sexual aim is the 'discharge of sexual products'. On the other hand, he suggests that the unfortunate girls are attacked by a fresh wave of suppression, because they have to overcome their previous 'masculine' sexuality and transfer the erotogenic zone from the clitoris to the vagina. This process is very difficult, and apparently takes place during what Freud referred to rather obscurely as a period of anaesthesia in the young woman. If this process is not properly completed, and the clitoris remains the main focus of sexual excitation, it is a frequent cause of neurosis, especially hysteria.

Freud's theories on female sexuality and development now seem highly dubious and confused. However, it is important to remember that he developed these theories nearly a hundred years ago, when female sexuality was very poorly understood. Astoundingly, the true structure and function of the clitoris has only very recently been revealed. This lack of understanding was not really because Freud was sexist – it simply reflects the general lack of understanding that people had at the time. There is a fascinating snippet in one of his letters to Wilhelm Fliess, dated 15 October 1897, which indicates strongly that he was actually very interested in exploring the psychology of both men and women and the ways in which they overlap. In this letter he is talking about his self-analysis and complains of experiencing a block in his exploration, which lasted for three days. He had a feeling of being 'tied up inside' – a feeling that his patients had often complained to him about. Then, on the fourth day, things began to flow smoothly again. He was baffled by all this until he realized that a similar block had occurred 28 days before. From this he concludes that what he refers to as the 'female period' is not conducive to doing analytical work. This suggests that he is exploring the idea that the male psyche has important female aspects within it – an interesting idea that was surely way ahead of his time.

According to Freud, childhood and puberty are fraught with sexual pitfalls and one false step along the way can lead to any number of problems in later life, as discussed below.

INCEST

The object choice begins with the child's early relationships with parents and carers. It is only later diverted away to other people by incest taboos. Freud says that sometimes the parents' natural affection for a child may awaken sexual interest too soon. On the other hand, if this can be avoided, then the emotional support of the parents will help the child towards choosing an appropriate sexual object when maturity is reached. Perhaps then the simplest choice would seem to be for the child to choose one of the parents as a sexual object – after all, since early childhood the parents have been associated with a kind of damped-down libido.

However, in reality this is not the best choice because the cultural demands of society prevent incest. The latency period allows the child to learn about these rules, and is followed at puberty by the teenage rebellion period, when the child gradually loosens the connection with the parents. In some cases this process goes wrong and the child is unable to overcome the sense of parental authority and may persist in childish affection for the parents long after puberty. Freud says that this is particularly common, even encouraged, among girls. Even if a person manages to avoid an incestuous relationship, he or she may still fall in love for the first time with a much older person. This echoes the earlier relationship with the mother or father.

FIXATION

The child can get stuck at any stage in the sexual development process. This is called **fixation**. Freud says that in some cases it is possible to trace a connection between a character trait and specific erotogenic components. For example, obstinacy, thrift and orderliness are linked with anal eroticism, while ambition is determined by strong urethral eroticism. He attributed a great many of the sexual deviations that he met in clinical practice to fixations caused by early impressions in childhood.

REPRESSION

Repression of sexual urges may lead to psychoneurotic illness, such as the perversions we looked at earlier. Freud emphasized that repressing an urge was not the same thing as abolishing it. Instead, the urge is prevented by psychical blocks from attaining its aim. It may then be diverted into numerous other channels, and find its way to the surface as neurotic symptoms. The affected person may then be able to lead a comparatively normal, often somewhat restricted sexual life, but will tend to suffer from psychoneurotic illness.

SUBLIMATION

Very often the libido finds an outlet in another, non-sexual field. This is called sublimation (see Chapter 5). According to Freud, sublimation is one of the origins of artistic ability: on analysis, people who are gifted creatively often prove to have various sexual deviations and neurotic symptoms. In fact, Freud sees a person's whole character as being built to a considerable extent by sublimation and other constructions that keep perverse impulses under control.

Freud suggests that neurotic people may have a greater tendency to be affected by early sexual experiences, and a greater tendency to become fixated. He saw one of the main causes of fixation to be the early seduction of the child by another child or an adult. He suggested that sexual deviations could arise through a combination of several causes:

- ▶ *a compliant constitution and/or precocity*
- ▶ *increased susceptibility to early sexual experiences*

▶ *chance stimulation of the sexual instinct by external influences, such as a foot fetish brought about by an early encounter with velvet slippers.*

However, it is not easy to sort out the extent to which constitutional or external factors are responsible for sexual deviations. Freud said that in exploring the theory of sexuality people are always liable to overestimate the former, whereas in clinical practice the latter tend to be given more emphasis.

Although Freud continued to explore sexual disturbances all his life, he was frustrated by his lack of knowledge about the biological processes underlying sexual behaviour. He claimed that this lack of knowledge prevented him from ever being able to formulate a really adequate theory about how normal sexuality developed and pathological conditions arose. But he maintained that one of the most important results of his psychoanalytic research was the discovery that neurotic anxiety arises out of the transformation of unacceptable libidinal urges.

THINGS TO REMEMBER

Freud's views on sexuality, particularly that of infants, caused great uproar amongst his contemporaries.

Freud said that:

▶ *The sexual instinct was a lot more complicated than people had previously maintained.*

▶ *Sexual impulses are present from birth, but are soon overcome by a progressive process of repression.*

▶ *The sexuality of neurotics and deviants has usually remained in, or been brought back to, an infantile state.*

▶ *Childhood and puberty are fraught with sexual pitfalls and development can go wrong or get stuck at any stage. This is called fixation.*

▶ *One of the main causes of fixation is early seduction by another child or by an adult.*

7

Going back to childhood

In this chapter you will learn:
- *what Freud thought about infantile amnesia*
- *in more depth about Freud's theories of psychosexual development*
- *the theory behind the Oedipus complex.*

Psychosexual development

> **Insight**
> Psychosexual: relating to the mental aspects of sex, such as sexual fantasies.

The idea current when Freud was writing was that children have no sexual instinct until puberty. When occasional references were made in literature to sexual activity in children, such as masturbation, these were quoted as exceptional and horrifying oddities. Freud attacked this notion that children were essentially asexual as being a grave error, because it prevents people from understanding sexuality properly at all. He suggested that a proper study of childhood sexuality would reveal not only the essential characteristics of the sexual instinct, but also the way in which it develops and what influences it.

Freud gradually developed his ideas about childhood sexuality in order to try and explain how people develop into social beings.

His theories about childhood sexuality are really, therefore, part of an attempt at a much broader theory of human personality. Eventually, psychoanalytical thinking divided psychosexual development into several definite stages. Each stage followed on from the one before in a biologically determined manner, and the way a person coped with each stage influenced their adult personality. Freud did not explain these stages all at once in a neat and logical order, but added to his theories over a period of many years. The ideas are therefore scattered in different parts of his writing, but a lot of them are explained in the second essay of *Three Essays on the Theory of Sexuality*, first published in 1905.

From birth onwards, instincts or drives compel the infant to seek bodily/sexual pleasure. The development of the personality depends on progressing through various stages of psychosexual growth in which this is accomplished in different ways. Each stage is concerned with ways in which children experience sexual pleasure at that particular phase of development. Sexuality is a dominant theme in Freud's work and he was very much concerned with the ways in which the libido can become blocked or redirected. Although he soon rejected the seduction theory as the cause of all adult neurosis, he did continue to believe that neurosis was connected with problems in sexual development and functioning.

Freud suggested that there were two main characteristics of infantile sexuality:

▶ *It is essentially autoerotic, finding its object in the child's own body.*
▶ *It is made up of individual component instincts, each of which follows its own course in the search for pleasure.*

If everything goes according to plan, then sexual development in the child leads to a normal adult sexual life. In adulthood, the pursuit of sexual pleasure is controlled by the reproductive system, which harnesses the various component instincts of the sexual drive for the pursuit of a definite sexual aim, attached to an external sexual object.

Because the child's attempts to satisfy the pleasure drive are often met with disapproval and punishment, the developmental process leads the child through a whole series of conflicts. Normally the adult stage is reached smoothly; however, things can go wrong, and a person can get stuck at a particular stage in sexual development. This is what Freud refers to as fixation. It can occur at any of the various stages of development and it leads to pathological problems in later life that give rise to neurotic symptoms and behaviour. In some people fixation is relatively permanent, so that further psychosexual development becomes impossible. In other cases, usually as a result of stress of some kind, people will go back to behaving as they did at an earlier stage of development. This is called 'regression' and often occurs as a result of fixation.

Infantile amnesia

Freud suggests that the main reason people were convinced that children had no sexual feelings is that they had actually forgotten the events of their own childhoods. In 1916 he coined the phrase 'infantile amnesia' to describe this curious phenomenon of forgetting our earliest memories.

He believed that it was very important to gain understanding of this phenomenon because early memories, if we could only unlock them, held the key to understanding all adult behaviour, from 'normal' behaviour right through to that of neurotic and even psychotic people.

Freud said that in most of us the phase of infantile amnesia hides the earliest beginnings of childhood up until the age of six or eight years. It is true that in most people there seems to be a state of amnesia that blocks early memories right up until the sixth or eighth year of life. Recent studies have shown that most people cannot remember anything at all before the age of about three and a half, although girls tend to remember further back than boys.

Up until the age of eight most people still have fewer memories than they can recall for later periods of life.

Why, then, should the function of memory apparently lag so far behind the other functions in the developing psyche? After all, it is obvious that small children can see and hear perfectly well, and react to stimuli.

Insight

Infantile amnesia: a lot of confusion has arisen because studies in the past have tended to focus on adults, who are often unable to remember much about their early childhood. In actual fact recent research has shown that very small children *do* remember events, but these memories are not always retained into adulthood.

Freud says that what is actually going on is not a real erasing of early memory traces, it is in fact a state of deliberately *withholding* these impressions from consciousness. Freud called this process repression. A similar repression process is seen in neurotic patients in connection with events in later life. But what forces bring about this repression? Freud says that if we could solve this riddle then we could probably explain hysterical amnesia as well. Because he laid great emphasis on sexual repression as the main cause of hysterical symptoms, then it was a logical step to suggest that infantile amnesia was also caused by repression of sexual impulses. Freud claims that early sexual impulses are taboo and frightening because they are directed towards the child's parents, and so cannot be held intact in the psyche and have to be suppressed.

Freud said that early sexual urges were often disguised by neutral and innocuous 'screen memories'. He describes one of his own persistent childhood memories in this way. In this memory he is playing in a field of flowers, accompanied by two of his half-brother's children, John and Pauline. Freud says that this innocent memory conceals the neurotic need he felt for a male playmate and also the unacceptable competitive and aggressive urges that he knew would arise if this wish were granted.

He recalled that the arrival of his own younger brother had been greeted with adverse wishes and profound jealousy. When this brother subsequently died, Freud was left with a huge sense of guilt.

Freud's theory about screen memories tends to fall down for two reasons:

- ▶ *In fact, traumatic or disturbing memories of early childhood are just as common as in later periods of life.*
- ▶ *It does not explain why there is a general state of infantile amnesia – what happens to all the neutral or pleasant memories about everyday events?*

Freud thought that the period of infantile amnesia was necessary to the development of a healthy psyche because it was essential to block out material of a sexual and aggressive nature that was directed towards the parents. Only then could a person have a normal adult sex life. This idea is interesting in the light of Freud's own death wish towards his father, and it shows that once again he was tending to generalize on the basis of flimsy data.

Freud maintained that if the sex drive was allowed to be expressed openly, all sorts of wild fantasies and childish passions would burst forth and the person would begin to act out their sexual and aggressive urges. Neurotic symptoms arise when the repression process fails and hidden urges begin to rise to the surface of the unconscious. The aim of psychotherapy was to try to take the person back into childhood to examine hidden repressed memories in the light of adult, logical thinking, so that they would then lose their hold over the psyche.

As was so often the case, Freud's ideas about infantile amnesia were rather vague and ambiguous. As well as suggesting that screen memories were put in place, he also suggested that there was a process of selective reconstruction going on. The idea is that we cannot remember very much from childhood because the actual method of processing information in the brain has changed.

This seems somewhat closer to the truth in the light of modern experimental psychology, but there is still disagreement as to what might cause such a change in mental processing.

More modern research is still shedding light on the phenomenon of infantile amnesia, and many psychologists are coming to the conclusion that it does not really exist. Some people can remember events from the very early period of their lives, and many of these memories show that small children have definite emotions and are capable of insight and judgement. Some people believe that all the memories are still there somewhere; it is just a case of finding a trigger to unearth them. Certainly some people are able to recall early childhood events under hypnosis, although this leads to another dilemma in trying to find out if such memories are genuine. But babies as young as one year old show perfectly normal long- and short-term recall, and are able to find hidden objects and so on. What they cannot do at this stage is describe their memories verbally and it is here that a partial explanation for the amnesia may lie.

The oral stage

Freud identifies two 'pregenital' stages of sexual development. These are the oral and anal stages, which he suggests almost seem to hark back to earlier forms of animal life. The oral stage is the first stage of psychosexual development and it lasts from birth to about one year old. Freud gives it an alternative name – the cannibalistic stage. At this stage all the infant's libidinal desire is orientated towards the lips and the mouth. The aim is to ingest milk, food, and almost anything else that comes to hand – babies are always putting everything into their mouths. Because sexual activity is not yet separated from the ingestion of food, the sexual aim is *incorporation* of the object. The infant also indulges in auto-erotic stimulation, sucking various parts of the body, especially the thumb. This activity obviously develops from sucking the mother's breast. The sucking is rhythmic, and often involves rubbing movements as well. Freud says that these lead on to masturbation later. The activity is very absorbing and comforting and often sends the infant off to sleep.

Sucking is obviously by far the most important activity at this stage in the baby's life, and so the mother's breast becomes the first love/sex object. The baby feels love or hate for the mother accordingly, as the breast is offered or withdrawn. This dual aspect of the love object – bringing both pleasure and pain – is common to later stages of sexual development as well. The source of love at the oral stage is also the food source, and it gradually becomes a source of sexual pleasure. Freud broadened the concept of sexual pleasure, allowing it to encompass what is now usually called sensual pleasure.

Withdrawal of the breast is seen as withdrawal of love. Fixation at this stage is called 'oral fixation' by Freud, who says that this fixation sometimes occurs when babies have not been breast-fed. It manifests in the adult in all sorts of ways, for example:

▶ *thumb sucking in older children*
▶ *chewing gum, pens, pencils, finger nails, etc.*
▶ *smoking, over-eating or over-drinking*
▶ *feeling a constant need to be loved*
▶ *passivity and over-dependence.*

This seems to cover the vast majority of the adult population, so presumably we are not very good at getting past this first stage.

The anal stage

This is the second stage, and Freud gives it the alternative name of the 'sadistic-anal' phase. It lasts from about the age of one to three years, and coincides with the potty training phase, when the child learns to control the bladder and bowels. The child feels very proud when it produces stools and often sees them as part of itself. Because they are a product of his own body, the child sees the faeces as a kind of precious gift, but to his surprise the reaction of his parents or carers is not what he expects! The adults who care for the child may express disgust, especially if the child produces offerings at an inappropriate time or place, or tries to handle his gift, or smear it around the place. So the child has to learn when producing faeces is socially acceptable and when it is not, and also that it is 'dirty' to handle them.

The child soon finds that it can gain power over the adult by withholding stools, or by producing them at the wrong time. According to Freud, producing or withholding stools is all very pleasurable. When potty training begins, the baby often deliberately hangs onto its stools because it wants to enjoy the erotic pleasure of producing the stool in private! Producing a huge stool also apparently causes a wonderful stimulation of the mucous membrane of the anus. (A more acceptable argument today is that stool retention happens because the baby is constipated and producing huge compacted stools is painful.)

Freud says that by the time of the anal stage, opposition has already developed between the two currents that run through all sexual life. These two opposing energies cannot yet be described as masculine and feminine, but merely as active and passive. The first is represented in the urge to control the muscles of the anus, the second in the stimulation of the erotogenic mucous membrane.

There is another aspect to this duality: the child can either conform and produce the stool at the right time and place, or it can wield power by withholding the stool or producing it at an inopportune moment. The anal phase is the time when social conditioning really begins to come into play. The child is praised for being 'clean' and getting things 'right'. On the other hand, repressive guilt and disgust begin to appear when the child gets it 'wrong'. Fixation at this stage can take more than one form:

▶ Anal expulsiveness *follows on from producing stools inappropriately. Adults stuck at this stage are often scruffy, disordered and anti-social. Interestingly, our language reflects the connection between the anti-social character and faeces with phrases such as 'he's a real shit'.*

▶ Anal retentiveness *follows on from withholding stools. The adult stuck at this stage is compulsively neat and tidy, orderly and conformist, and there is a close association with money and miserliness, because of the sense of trying to hang on to possessions. This is because the psyche still retains a dim memory of the early childhood belief that the faeces are a precious gift. Again, our language reflects the connection between money and faeces with phrases such as 'filthy rich' and, 'where there's muck there's brass'. Obstinate people are also stuck at this stage because they are rebelling against the parental insistence that there is a correct time and place to produce a stool.*

▶ *Parental disapproval at the anal stage can also lead to a later neurotic obsession with dirt and cleaning.*

Freud's assumption about the existence of the two pregenital sexual phases is based on his analysis of neuroses. He suggests that further work of this kind would provide more information about the structure and development of normal sexual functioning.

Passing on the anal fixation.

The phallic stage

This stage is from the age of about three to five years, and involves the third and final erotogenic zone of infancy. The genitals – that is the penis or the clitoris – now become the erogenous zone and masturbation begins. Initially, Freud thought that early sexual awakening in this area must usually involve some deliberate involvement on the part of another person, such as a parent, sibling or nurse. But later he decided that a lot of the early childhood seduction scenes related to him by patients were actually fantasies, cooked up at a later stage in order to block out a real memory, as he describes happening in the case of his famous patient the Wolf Man (see Chapter 10).

Freud eventually decided that the child has a natural tendency to explore his own body. In addition to this, the infant genital zone is stimulated frequently by washing, rubbing dry, urinating and so on. The child soon learns to stimulate the area itself, by rubbing with the hand or by pressing the thighs together. The child becomes fascinated by urination, and derives pleasure from both retaining and expelling urine. Freud's views on this stage reveal a misogynist attitude – the phallus is seen as all-important. In fact, he almost seems to regard it as the only sexual organ, saying (rather obscurely) that for both sexes only the phallus counts. However, he does admit that he can only describe what happens in little boys, because the corresponding process in girls is not known to him.

At first the male child assumes that everybody has the same genital apparatus as himself, i.e. a penis. He can see that men and women are different, but he has no reason to suppose that there is any difference in genitalia. (Remember that in Freud's day everybody was decently covered all the time.) But the phallic stage is when sexual differences are often discovered by children, by chance glimpses of genitalia, or through observing others urinating. This shocking revelation gives rise to the castration complex in boys and penis envy in girls (see Chapter 6).

At first the little boy goes into denial when he discovers that girls do not have a penis. He tells himself that there is a penis there really, that it will get bigger in due course and so on. Then slowly, he comes to the horrid conclusion that there must have been a penis there to begin with and it has been taken away – hence the castration complex. But, he reasons to himself this cannot be true of all females, it has only happened to females who have had bad sexual thoughts (like himself) and had therefore needed to be punished by castration. Therefore, being a woman does not necessarily equal not having a penis. Meanwhile, girls see themselves as already castrated and never really recover from the shock of the revelation about penises.

Later, when the little boy realizes that only women can have babies, he also understands that all women lack a penis, so the penis has in fact somehow been exchanged for a baby. Freud claimed that all children believe at this stage that they can either give their mother a baby, or else produce one themselves by giving birth anally. These curious theories perhaps serve to underline the dangers of trying to evolve theories about normal child development from working with neurotic adults! This is also the stage when the notorious Oedipus complex emerges.

Fixation at the phallic stage could perhaps be reflected in someone who brags about sex and sees it as a way of gaining power over others. Such a person is not really capable of forming a proper relationship with the opposite sex.

The Oedipus complex

Freud formed his ideas about the Oedipus complex during the period of his own self-analysis. In a letter to Fliess at this time (dated 15 October 1897), he describes discovering that as a small boy he had been in love with his mother and jealous of his father. He soon decided that this was, in fact, an almost universal occurrence in small children and he came to view it as the central phenomenon of the sexual period of early childhood.

The basic problem that arises for the child is that he has a secret passionate love for his mother which cannot be fulfilled for fear of offending his father. This passion cannot remain innocent, because the child soon comes to link his own sexual excitement about his mother with parental disapproval and his own feelings of jealousy. (More about what happens for girls later!)

The Oedipus complex is named after a character in an ancient Greek story. Oedipus was the son of King Laius and Queen Jocasta of Thebes. It was prophesied that Oedipus would murder his father and marry his mother, so to avoid this his father had him left exposed to die on the mountain soon after his birth. However, the baby was rescued and brought up by strangers.

Eventually, Oedipus met his father by chance on the road to Thebes and murdered him in a fit of rage. He then went to Thebes and rid the city of a tiresome Sphinx who had been eating anybody who was unable to answer her riddle correctly. Oedipus answered the riddle and was rewarded by being made king, and so ended up unknowingly marrying his mother Jocasta, who was still queen. Eventually, Oedipus found out what he had unknowingly done, and blinded himself as a punishment before wandering off and living out his life in exile.

Freud says that:

▶ *At the height of the phallic phase all little boys of about four or five fall in love with their mothers.*
▶ *The boy expresses his desire in various ways, such as by announcing that he is going to marry her, or by insisting on climbing into bed with her all the time.*
▶ *He becomes very curious about her naked body.*

- *The boy wants total possession of the mother and so he becomes very jealous of his father and wants to kill him to get him out of the way.*
- *Because the father is obviously so big and powerful, the boy is afraid that he will be punished by his father castrating him. This fear arises out of the 'castration complex', which forms when the child is ticked off for masturbating and warned that his penis might drop off and/or has already observed the fact that girls seem to be 'missing' a penis.*
- *The fear of the father's reprisal in this way eventually makes the boy abandon his mother as a sexual object. Instead, he now begins to identify himself with his potentially aggressive father and begins to look elsewhere for a sexual partner.*

The picture Freud paints for girls is even more bizarre and he is typically much less clear about his views:

- *The little girl is also involved with lusting after the mother initially, but then comes the awful revelation that boys have a penis and she does not.*
- *The little girl believes she has lost hers and (for some obscure reason) blames her mother for this.*
- *The little girl cannot fear castration because she sees herself as already castrated. For her, the corresponding fear is the loss of love.*
- *She then turns to the father as a sex object, hoping that he will impregnate her. The resulting baby would partly make up for the lost penis.*
- *The conflict is gradually resolved as she turns her attention away from her father towards other men who will be able to provide her with a baby.*

Quite how Freud thinks this last stage happens in women is a bit vague and reflects the fact that Freud didn't really understand women's psychology very well. After all, he had arrived at his theories about the Oedipus complex mainly through his own self-analysis.

OEDIPUSS PUSS PUSS...

The author's Oedipus complex develops new complications following a visit to her grandparents.

Insight

Freud didn't seem to understand little girls very well at all, which may seem strange considering that he had sisters and then later on daughters of his own. But one has to remember that female psychology, especially in relation to sexuality, was very little understood in Freud's time.

Freud saw the Oedipal conflict as being basic to psychosexual development. Failure to resolve this incestuous conflict would result in neurosis later in life. To us today the theory can all seem rather contrived, but this is partly because it has been overstated by Freud and he seems to make the mistake of generalizing on the basis of his own childhood experiences. However, if we look at the theory again we can see some elements of truth in it, for example:

- *Small boys do sometimes seem to fall in love with their mothers, and may consequently get very jealous of the father.*
- *The same can be true with small girls and their fathers.*

▶ *The blinding of Oedipus is symbolic of the shock, self-disgust and self-punishment that may arise when dark inner wishes are revealed. Many people do feel guilty about their own natural sexual urges.*

▶ *Men and boys sometimes do fear castration or damage to the penis – the male genitalia are rather vulnerable after all. In the past, little boys were actually threatened with having their penis cut off if they masturbated, which would obviously lead to considerable anxiety.*

▶ *In Freud's day, girls were seen as being inferior, and making a baby was probably one of the few important things they felt they could do.*

The latency stage

According to Freud the feelings from the Oedipal stage are eventually suppressed and the sexual drive goes dormant from about the age of five until puberty. Up until now the little boy has regarded his mother as his sole property, but he now realizes that he has to share her attention with his father and with other siblings too. Probably because of his own childhood experiences, Freud seems to assume that these are younger siblings who have arrived after the child himself and claimed the mother's attention. Similarly the little girl likes to imagine that she is the centre of her father's universe, but sooner or later this illusion is also shattered.

During the latency stage, the child gradually begins to free itself from this utter dependence on the parents. The Oedipus complex is slowly resolved as the child distances itself from the mother and reconciles itself with the father. During this phase, sexual impulses and behaviour are much less in evidence, although not entirely abolished. In fact, subsequent research has shown that this is not really the case; on the contrary, sexual curiosity, sexual play and masturbation all gradually increase. However, they may be concealed from adults if the child is not living in a permissive family, which may have been the case in Freud's time.

The genital stage

The final stage in development is the genital stage, which is from puberty onwards. There is now a renewal of sexual interest after the latency stage, and a new object is found for the sex drive. If all has developed according to plan, the individual is now less centred on the self and becomes capable of a satisfying relationship with a member of the opposite sex. The Oedipus complex is now resolved and the natural aim of the sex drive becomes sexual intercourse with an opposite-sex adult.

This is seen as the final stage, the completion of development, which seems rather odd considering the angst and confusion most of us go through in our teens and early adulthood! Really, however, Freud recognized this in pointing out that even in the most mature and well-balanced individual it is often possible to detect traces of the earlier stages of sexual development. In cases of neurosis, early repression leaves part of the person's sexuality underdeveloped. In cases of perversion on the other hand, the opposite happens – a part of the sexual instinct becomes over-exaggerated and the person acts on it in real life. So this means that both neurotics and perverts have become fixated at an early stage of sexual development, but they have dealt with this fixation in very different ways.

Freud insisted that psychosexual development was central to all social and emotional development. He argued that if one persisted long enough in analysis of any adult one would ultimately get past any current trauma to unveil repressed sexual problems from childhood. Far from being disinterested in sex, children were always exploring their own bodies and were also fascinated, aroused and frequently disturbed when they happened to witness adults having sex. Freud believed that his new theories about the way the child's sexuality developed provided a model of the way the whole personality developed. However, he did not actually say that the *whole* mind was *only* concerned with sex, since if it were there would be no conflicts. A lot of the

opposition to his theories has arisen because of the way
he defined what 'sexual' meant. For him the concept had a
much broader meaning than just sex itself; nevertheless, most
people now feel that he overemphasized the sexual element of
human nature.

THINGS TO REMEMBER

▶ *Freud's definition of what was sexual was very broad.*

▶ *He said that children had sexual experiences right from birth.*

▶ *According to Freud the phase of infantile amnesia hides early sexual experiences.*

▶ *Freud's theories about how children developed sexually became a model for social and psychological development in general.*

▶ *Normal sexual development was seen as going through definite stages that were the same in all children.*

▶ *Each stage was concerned with a different source of sexual pleasure.*

▶ *People could get stuck at any stage – this was called fixation.*

▶ *Behaviour could also hark back to an earlier stage – this was called regression.*

▶ *Fixation and regression led to neurotic problems or perversions in adult life.*

8

Seeking an adult identity

In this chapter you will learn:
- *key features of Freud's new model of how the mind works*
- *theories about how the mind defends itself*
- *in more depth about how the adult character develops.*

Freud's new model of the mind

In the previous chapter we looked at Freud's ideas about how the adult personality develops and what can go wrong with this process. He also gradually developed theories about the ways in which the personality is actually formed and structured. For a long time he struggled with the problem of how neuroses arose. He knew that unacceptable or frightening ideas were repressed and banished to the unconscious, but where did this repression come from?

The original simple division of the mind into conscious and unconscious did not fully explain what was going on, so in 1923 Freud published his book *The Ego and the Id*, which proposed a new **dynamic model** of the mind.

> **Insight**
> A dynamic model is a simplified description of a system, emphasizing forces, motives and drives. It shows us how a thing works.

This was an attempt to describe the whole mind system, explaining how it works, and what are its main motives and drives. It involved three main parts: the id, ego and super-ego. These are not really physical parts of the brain but represent different aspects of the way we think, and so help to explain the apparent battle that goes on between different levels of consciousness. Freud didn't see them with exact boundaries like countries on a map, but rather as merging into one another, like the areas of colour mixed together by an artist. They did not *replace* the idea of conscious/unconscious – as we shall see later, they can sometimes operate on both levels.

Insight

Id: the unconscious part of the psyche that is concerned with inherited, instinctive impulses.

Ego: the part of the psyche which reacts to external reality and which a person thinks of as the 'self'.

Super-ego: the part of the psyche that acts like an 'inner parent', giving us a conscience and responding to social rules.

Freud explained that he was really suggesting new ways of looking at the psyche and the way in which it was arranged, rather than making startling new discoveries. Like so much of Freud's thinking, this was an ongoing process, so he constantly revised and modified what he thought to be true. This fact, coupled with the fact that the subject matter is somewhat abstract in any case, makes his ideas hard to grasp at times.

In exploring the way the mind is structured, Freud justified his use of clinical data from his work with patients by use of an analogy. If we throw a crystal on the floor, it tends to break along predetermined lines of weakness, inherent in its structure. Mental patients are split and broken in the same way, showing us the way the psyche is constructed. And the fact that they tend to turn away from external reality means that they know more about internal, psychical reality than most people, and so they can reveal things to us that would otherwise remain hidden.

Insight

'Id', 'ego' and 'super-ego' were not actually Freud's original words. He used words that can be translated as 'the It', 'the I' and 'the Over-I', which were perhaps rather more self-explanatory.

The id

From the Latin word for 'it', the id is the primitive, unconscious part of the mind that we are born with. The other parts of the mind are derived from this oldest, primeval part, which contains everything that is inherited. It is a dark, inaccessible area, seething with instinctive urges and its only reality is its own selfish needs. It is the source of the motive force behind the pleasure principle which involves avoiding states of tension or 'unpleasure', caused by the thwarting of a basic drive. In the young infant this is all about having its needs met immediately – as anyone who has looked after a baby for any length of time will know, the child will scream whenever it is hungry, or even the slightest bit uncomfortable in any way. So the id is concerned with simple biology and the basic needs of the organism.

As a child develops through the various oral, anal and phallic stages, it begins to realize that the world 'out there' is real too. This new awareness is closely linked to sexual development. Gradually, the child begins to realize that it cannot always instantly have what it wants, and begins to suppress the id urges in order to fit in with society. Adults who are very selfish or impulsive may be unable or unwilling to suppress the id.

The id is disorganized and illogical in nature, and much of its content is negative and selfish. It can make no value judgements – it is completely amoral. The desires of the id are commonly expressed in dreams and what little we know about it is partly gained from the study of dreams and partly from looking at neurotic symptoms. It uses a form of mental functioning that Freud called primary process, which involves the various mechanisms such as symbolization, condensation and so on discussed in Chapter 4. Because it is not logical, it ignores basic rational rules such as time and space, giving rise to the strange illogical fantasy world that most people are familiar with from their dreams.

Because the id has no concept of time it contains impulses and impressions that may have arisen from events that occurred decades before, but which still affect the person as if they were happening in the present. These can only be recognized as belonging to the past when they are made conscious by the work of analysis. Only then can they lose their importance and stop affecting the person's thinking and behaviour.

The ego

Named from the Latin word for 'I', the ego is the part of the mind that reacts to external reality and which a person thinks of as the 'self'. The ego is where consciousness comes from, although not all of its functions are carried out consciously.

▶ *The ego tells us what is real. It is a synthesizer – it helps us to combine ideas and make sense of things.*
▶ *It is practical and rational, involved in decision making.*
▶ *Anxiety arises from the ego. This is seen as a mechanism for warning us that there is a weakness somewhere in the ego's defences.*
▶ *The ego can observe itself – in fact, in a number of its functions it can split temporarily and then come together again afterwards.*
▶ *A whole system of unconscious* **defence mechanisms** *protects the ego. These are involuntary or unconscious ways of protecting the ego from undesirable feelings and emotions.*
▶ *The ego is seen as being rather weak in comparison with the id, but it is better organized and more logical, so that it usually maintains a tenuous upper hand.*

Defence mechanisms are unconscious ways of protecting the
ego against undesirable effects. They help us to cope with
the anxieties of life, and defend our self-image. Sometimes
of course they are overdone, and then they can lead to
problems. For example we have all met people who are
'over-defensive' and end up becoming aggressive.

Freud explains, somewhat confusingly, that the ego is part of the id
that develops in order to cope with threats from the outside world.
It is related to the system he refers to as the 'perceptual-conscious',
which he sees as the most superficial portion of the mental apparatus.
This could be described as a kind of protective skin which provides us
with external perceptions at the same time as giving information about
what is going on in the interior mind. This information is essential
for the id because otherwise it would ignore the influence of the outer
world and eventually be destroyed in one way or another in its blind
pursuit of selfish satisfaction. For example, you need to learn that you
can't just dash across the road to a cake shop without first checking to
see if you will get run over by a bus. In other words, the main function
of the ego is that of reality testing: it replaces the primitive pleasure
principle of the id with a new reality principle, which ultimately
promises more certainty and greater success in accomplishing goals.

Freud compares the ego and the id with a rider and his horse. The
horse supplies the motor energy, but the rider decides where to go.
The ego constantly has to devise little plans to satisfy the id in a
controlled way. For example, a child is hungry but learns that it will
have to wait until teatime until it gets a slice of cake. The problem-
solving and reality-testing activities of the ego, which allow the id to
take care of its needs as soon as an appropriate object can be found,
are what Freud referred to as secondary process.

The super-ego

Some of Freud's patients suffered from delusions of being watched.
Freud suggests that in a sense they were right, and that in each of

us there is an agency that observes our behaviour and threatens to punish us – a sort of inner grown-up. In the delusional patients, this agency could simply have become sharply divided from the ego and mistaken for external reality.

A very young child is amoral and has little sense of inhibition. Any controls over its behaviour are provided by the parents and other carers who look after it. In normal development this state of affairs slowly changes. As the ego struggles to keep the id happy, it constantly meets up with both obstacles and helpers in the external world. It keeps a track record of these, and also of rewards and punishments that it has encountered, particularly from parents and other adults. This is how the super-ego develops: gradually a sort of inner parent evolves and the child develops feelings of guilt and of being watched and controlled. One aspect of this super-ego is what we would call the conscience – the part of ourselves that tells us what is right and what is wrong and judges our behaviour accordingly; but the super-ego also carries out self-observation, which is an essential preliminary to the judging process.

This is the work of the super-ego:

▶ *It gives us our sense of right and wrong, pride and guilt.*
▶ *It often gets us to act in ways that are acceptable to the society, rather than to the individual. For example, it might make a person feel guilty for having extra-marital sex. The super-ego incorporates the teachings of the past and of tradition, imparting a sense of morals.*
▶ *It monitors behaviour, decides what is acceptable and controls taboo areas, by means of repression. The fact that a person may not be aware of this repression shows that parts of the super-ego can operate unconsciously. In fact, Freud says that large parts of both the ego and the super-ego are normally unconscious.*
▶ *It allows the ego to measure itself and strive towards ever-greater perfection.*
▶ *It is rather bossy, always demanding perfection of the ego. In fact, it can be quite severe with the poor ego, humiliating it, ill-treating it and threatening it with dire punishments. Freud observed this sort of thing in his melancholic patients.*

The super-ego develops from and gradually takes the place of parental authority – observing, threatening and directing the ego in the same way as the parents did. Oddly, however, it seems to make a one-sided choice here, and seems not to regulate behaviour by means of loving care and encouragement. This is strange, given that the super-ego is all about what Freud calls the 'higher side' of human life and the striving towards perfection.

The super-ego develops as the Oedipus complex begins to be resolved, but if the resolution of the Oedipus complex is incomplete, the super-ego will remain stunted in its strength and growth and the child will remain over-identified with its parents. In the normal course of development, as the repression of Oedipal urges begins, the child feels a mixture of love, fear and hostility towards the parents.

The way the super-ego works is in a sense opposite to that of the id: the id just wants to satisfy the needs of the individual, regardless of what society wants. Like the ego, large parts of the super-ego can operate in unconscious ways. Freud acknowledges that the distinctions between id, ego and super-ego are not easy to grasp and that the three are not always sharply separated. If an adult has achieved a reasonably mature, mentally healthy personality, the id, ego and super-ego will be acting in a balanced way.

Freud explains that the child's super-ego is not really constructed on a model of the parents themselves, but rather of the parents' super-ego. In this sense it represents handed-down traditions and value judgements and so is a mirror for the workings of society itself. Freud defines a psychological group as a group of people who have introduced the same person into their super-ego and therefore, on the basis of this common element, identify with one another. Mankind never lives fully in the present, but is affected by inherited ideologies that are very slow to change. To understand the super-ego more fully would be to gain insight into many problems in the social behaviour of mankind, such as delinquency. Freud says that there is probably great variation among individuals in the development of the different parts of the psyche. The intention of psychoanalysis is really to strengthen the ego and make it more independent of the super-ego, so that it can widen its scope and take over fresh areas of the id. This is a huge task.

Anxiety

Conflicts between the different aspects of the personality result in anxiety and stress. Only the ego can produce and feel anxiety, which acts as an alarm signal that something is wrong. Anxiety can arise from blocked libido and thus give rise to repression.

Freud identified three types of anxiety:

▶ Realistic anxiety *arises from real events in the external world, perceived by the ego. It is associated with increased sensory attention and muscular tension. This is what we would normally call fear.*
▶ Neurotic anxiety *arises from impulses that are flooding from the id, and often seems enigmatic and unfocused. It is not necessarily connected with external events in the real world. It can be observed in three different conditions:*
  1 *as free floating, general apprehensiveness – 'something might happen'*
  2 *attached to certain ideas in so-called phobias – here the anxiety is exaggerated out of all proportion*
  3 *in hysteria and other forms of severe neurosis.*
▶ Moral anxiety *arises from the super-ego – it is the voice of the conscience, telling us when something is 'improper'. This kind of anxiety involves feelings of shame or guilt, and a fear of punishment.*

Anxiety from all three sources feels similar, and in fact anxiety can arise from a mixture of different sources at the same time. Anxiety is closely associated with feelings of guilt; it can also present itself in the form of phobias and hysteria. Hysterical anxiety can come as a very severe attack, which does not necessarily have an obvious source in the external world.

Freud says that the commonest cause of anxiety is sexual frustration. This begins in infancy, when the mother is not present, or the infant sees an unfamiliar face. (Remember that Freud says that the child sees the mother as the sex object at this stage – see Chapter 7.) In such circumstances the infant is not able to control his libidinal excitation and therefore converts it into anxiety. In adult life, anxiety shows up in cases of hysteria and other neuroses. Freud says that the process in the child and the adult is similar: in the adult process a portion of libido becomes unavailable, because it is attached to a repressed idea.

Freud observed a highly significant relation between the generation of anxiety and the formation of neurotic symptoms. For example, someone who suffers from agoraphobia (fear in and of open spaces) may begin by having an anxiety attack in the street. He later restricts the functioning of his ego by developing the agoraphobic symptoms, thus avoiding further anxiety attacks.

A particular source of anxiety is attached to each developmental stage. For example, at the phallic stage it is the fear of castration that causes anxiety, and at the latency stage it is a developing fear of the super-ego. As the ego gets stronger and more clearly defined the anxieties weaken, but traces of them usually remain. Neurotics remain infantile in their attitude to danger and consequently suffer a great deal of anxiety.

Defence mechanisms

Defence mechanisms arise in order to protect the ego from too much anxiety. Without them, the anxiety could become a threat to mental health, which would be counterproductive. So, by means of various defence mechanisms the ego blocks impulses, or distorts them into more acceptable and less threatening forms. Defence mechanisms are used unconsciously and within reason they are healthy. However, if they are over-active, they become damaging because they require a lot of mental effort to sustain them and mask issues that really need to be resolved. In fact they become a strategy for hiding from anxiety.

The term 'defence mechanism' covers a variety of behaviours observed by analysts, such as repression, forgetting things, and mannerisms such as nervous tics. Freud and others, such as his daughter Anna, identified many different defence mechanisms, some of which we will now have a look at.

REPRESSION

This is one of the most common defence mechanisms and forms the basis for many of Freud's theories. Undesirable information about a person, a situation, or an event becomes locked away in the unconscious, so repression is really a form of forgetting. The advantage of repression is that we do not have to deal with painful feelings and memories. People can lose whole blocks of time in this way after a traumatic event. Conscious efforts to recall events have no effect. This can apply both to emotional traumas and traumas caused by external events such as war. The disadvantage of repression is that we are denying reality, and this will eventually give rise to behavioural problems and symptoms such as phobias. Repression is often used in combination with other defence mechanisms.

DENIAL

Denial is closely related to repression, but this time the person refuses to accept the reality of a situation. This is sometimes acceptable as a short-term defence, but it becomes dangerous if the situation is never properly dealt with. For example, a person may find a suspicious lump somewhere on their body and, fearing it might be cancer, may forget all about it rather than going to the doctor. **Denial** may occur by itself or, like repression, in conjunction with other defence mechanisms.

Denial is often used by children, for example, a small child may come into the room with chocolate all round his mouth and adamantly deny having touched the birthday cake on the kitchen table. A closely related defence mechanism is denial in fantasy, which is also common in children and occurs when they turn the undesirable reality into something they can cope with, for example an aggressive father may be seen as a cuddly teddy bear.

Insight

Denial is a defence mechanism that everyone is familiar with. For example we talk about someone being 'in denial' when they have recently been bereaved and are not ready to accept the reality of the situation. This is another example of how Freud's ideas have become absorbed into everyday understanding.

DISPLACEMENT

Displacement is another common defence mechanism that arises as a result of repression. Because a person cannot release a basic feeling such as anger, it builds up and is then directed towards another person, animal or object that has nothing to do with the original situation. For example, a man may have a bad day at work and, rather than confront the boss, will go home and kick the dog or shout at the wife. In this way, the original impulse is directed onto a substitute target, which is seen as being safer in some way.

This can happen with love as well as anger; for example, someone who is unable to have a normal relationship with another human being may lavish all his affection on a pet. Sexual desire for a particular person may find a substitute object in a fetish.

Displacement can also appear passively, where the person constantly complains and demands attention. The mystifying, inscrutable silence conveying the unspoken message that one has 'done something' can be another of its unpleasant passive variations.

There is also a special form of displacement called 'turning against the self'. In this case, the substitute target is the self. Unfortunately, this usually happens with negative feelings that we refuse to acknowledge, such as hatred, contempt, anger and aggression. It gives rise to feelings of self-hatred, depression and inferiority. In more extreme cases this may lead to physical self-abuse.

PROJECTION

Projection is almost a combination of denial and displacement. It is once again a result of repression and is almost the opposite of turning against the self. This time the person is unable to recognize the reality of their own behaviour or feelings. The result is that taboo urges or faults are projected outwards onto another person. For example, the bossiest member of the household covers up by accusing one of the others of being bossy.

Projection.

....

Insight
Projection is a particularly interesting (and irritating!) defence mechanism whereby taboo urges or faults are attributed to someone else. It is often used as a means of sneakily shifting the blame.
....

Sometimes, when somebody complains frequently about a trait that they despise in other people it will be strongly present in their own psyche. So, the desires or faults are present in that person but can be denied because they have been identified in someone else. This can happen with group psychology as well as with individuals.

Closely related to projection is 'altruistic surrender', where a person tries to fulfil their needs vicariously, through other people. In extreme cases, most commonly in women, the person may lead their whole life putting other's needs before their own.

INTROJECTION

Also called 'identification', **introjection** involves absorbing someone else's personality characteristics into your own personality to compensate for some emotional shortfall. We have already met this mechanism, because it is actually the mechanism by which the super-ego develops. It is seen in small children who tell their cuddly animals not to be afraid of the dark. During the teenage years, this behaviour becomes very common when people identify with their favourite film stars or pop idols.

Insight

People whose ego boundaries are weak or as yet undefined (in other words their sense of self is poor) are more likely to use introjection as a defence mechanism.

A related mechanism – 'identification with the aggressor' – is a version of introjection that focuses on negative or feared traits. For example, a child may cope with growing up with an abusive father by covering up its fear and imitating the aggressive behaviour. An extreme example of this is Stockholm syndrome, named after a hostage crisis in Sweden when the hostages became very sympathetic towards their captors, rather than being angry at what they had done to them.

FANTASY

Most people indulge in a certain amount of fantasy and daydreaming in order to make life more bearable. This is perfectly normal and can actually be quite positive – for example, dreaming of that holiday in Spain might motivate you to work a little harder. It is only harmful when a person can no longer separate fantasy from reality. When this happens a person may spend so much psychic energy on fantasy that they do not address things that are blocking progress in real life.

RATIONALIZATION

Here a person finds an excuse for their behaviour that is more acceptable to the ego than the real reason. For example, the driver of a car might say: 'I took the wrong turning there because I was so busy trying to avoid that wretched cyclist who was all over the road.' This conveniently covers up the fact that actually they were not paying attention to where they were going in the first place. Some people can invent volumes of lies that neatly let them off the hook and allow them to avoid responsibility and guilt.

REGRESSION

Regression is another defence mechanism that we have already met. Here the person reverts back to an earlier behaviour or developmental stage that feels safe or comforting. We all tend to do it if we feel ill or upset. It is very common in children who want more attention, perhaps because of a new baby, or because their parents are getting divorced. Adults sometimes go into a severe regression after a ghastly trauma, and may even curl up into a foetal position.

Insight

Regression can even be fun, as any student will tell you at the end of final exams when everyone lets off steam in a very uninhibited way. But it can get overdone of course, in which case a person gets stuck in tiresome, infantile behaviour.

REACTION FORMATION

Sometimes a person feels an impulse and covers it up by displaying its exact opposite, for example, being polite to somebody they want to be rude to. **Reaction formation** is quite a common form of defence in teenagers and is often shown by an individual being hostile to somebody they are really attracted to. Another example is that of a person who cannot accept their own homosexual impulses becoming outwardly homophobic. The problem arises when the latent urge remains dormant and unresolved and so may build up into a powerfully negative force.

Insight

Reaction formations are cunning, confusing and often difficult to detect. The original impulse does not disappear, but is simply masked by the person behaving in the opposite manner. For example, someone who appears to be all love and light may turn out to be a total sadist.

UNDOING

This is a rather strange mechanism that makes us use special gestures or rituals in order to cancel out unpleasant thoughts or events after they have already occurred. For example, Freud describes a ritual of this sort used by his patient the Wolf Man, who had to breathe out noisily every time he encountered people he felt sorry for, such as beggars, old people or cripples, in order to avoid becoming like them. In 'normal' people this sort of undoing is usually more conscious and we may actually ask for forgiveness or carry out a special ritual of atonement, such as visiting a priest for confession.

ISOLATION

This is sometimes called intellectualization. The person who uses this mechanism strips all emotion from a threatening memory or impulse and gives the impression that it is of no consequence whatsoever. This commonly happens during an accident or emergency, but after the event the person becomes very upset. It may also happen following traumatic events from earlier in life, such as childhood abuse. Sometimes this mechanism is essential if the person is to continue functioning effectively, for example, doctors and nurses must employ it at the scene of emergencies that occur every day in the course of their work.

Isolation brings up an important point about defence mechanisms – they are all lies of one sort or another, even if we are not using them consciously. If we use them too often they build up until we can no longer separate fact from fantasy. Ultimately this may lead to a breakdown, as the ego can no longer cope with all the demands of the id and the super-ego. But we cannot live without defence mechanisms because there is simply too much to cope with in life without them.

SUBLIMATION

Freud suggested that this mechanism in particular should be seen as a positive defence. Sublimation involves transforming unacceptable impulses such as fear, aggression and sexual desire into socially acceptable forms. So a person who has deviant sexual desires might channel them into writing a novel, or someone who has struggled with their own emotional problems might become a psychotherapist!

Any of the defence mechanisms can be helpful and they all appear in the behaviour of normal healthy people. Problems only arise when they become too forceful and the person becomes blind to their true feelings and motives. The job of the psychoanalyst is to help people to unravel these feelings, which can be a very painful process but is one that can help a person become a more rounded adult.

Narcissism

Freud found some patients who did not respond to psychoanalytic therapy at all. He used the myth of Narcissus to explain this.

Narcissus was a beautiful youth in ancient Greece who fell in love with his own reflection in a pool. He pined away and eventually died and was turned into a flower because he could never fully possess himself. Freud saw this story as a good way of illustrating the idea of an ego that has become totally self-absorbed and can no longer relate to the outside world. Such cases of **psychosis** are not treatable by psychoanalysis, because the normal transference does not occur.

Narcissism is normal in infancy, when the infantile ego expects the outside world to be just the same as itself. It has its place in the normal adult psyche too, because we need to have a certain degree of self-esteem. We need to direct some of our libido towards the self (ego libido) and some towards others (object libido).
So even in a good, mutually supportive adult relationship, there is always some degree of narcissism involved. However, in some cases of mental illness the entire libido becomes directed towards the self and the person comes to think the whole world revolves around them. They may see themselves as omnipotent, or may become a hypochondriac, constantly worrying about their health and incapable of realizing that others have feelings too. Because narcissism is normal in very young infants, it can be regarded as a type or regression when it occurs in adults.

Mourning and melancholia

In 1915 Freud published a book called *Mourning and Melancholia*. Melancholia is what we would now call severe depression. This often occurs after a bereavement or divorce.

- *The person blames themself for what has happened and becomes very self-destructive, even suicidal.*
- *He or she becomes very withdrawn from the world, as in narcissism, but this time the self is seen as being bad, unworthy, dirty and so on.*
- *Severe mourning can conceal repressed hatred for the lost person. The lost person becomes identified with the patient's*

own ego, so that hate becomes self-hate and guilt. This is
called introjection and is one of the defence mechanisms
discussed above.

▶ *The person may regress to an infantile state, where biting,*
sucking and excreting are dominant. They may be absorbed
with images of excreta and filth.

All of these symptoms mean that the person does not have to
express their mixed feelings of love and hate directly.

The normal mourning state is what we all go through when we
have lost someone we love. It is similar to melancholia, but usually
less severe. It is quite normal for people in mourning to blame
themselves and feel that they did not put enough effort into the
relationship or give the lost person enough love. Mourning often
lasts a long time; Freud says that this is because it is difficult to
withdraw libido from any love object, and compares the situation
with the struggle neurotics often have breaking their Oedipal ties
to their parents.

Another difference between mourning and melancholia is that in
mourning the loss is fully conscious, whereas in melancholia it may
be partly unconscious. Melancholia also involves a greater loss of
self-esteem. Freud suggests that this is because people who react to
loss in this way are narcissistic and have chosen a love object that
is closely identified with the self. This means that losing the love
object is like losing a part of the ego.

Instincts

It is not always clear what Freud means when he talks about
'instincts'. In fact he says that they are a very vague concept,
'magnificent in their indefiniteness'. He complains that people are
forever inventing new instincts in order to explain different aspects
of behaviour such as love, hunger and aggression. Freud turned to
biology for help, trying as always to be scientific in his approach.

This was not easy, because science is concerned with external, observable reality, whereas Freud was grappling with the workings of the mind.

According to Freud, current biological thinking grouped instincts into two types, according to the aim of the behaviour involved. The first type was aimed at self-preservation, the second at preservation of the species. Freud carried this idea over into psychoanalysis and hence classified instincts in two ways:

▶ Ego instincts *are self-preserving and concerned with the needs of the individual.*
▶ Sexual instincts *are concerned with preserving the species and pertain to objects.*

Later, Freud decided that it was not necessary to separate the two, but that what was important was the degree to which libido was directed towards the self or to external objects.

Freud tried to clarify what he meant by an instinct by contrasting it with a stimulus. A stimulus, he said, arises from things going on outside the body. Instincts arise from within, so that one cannot avoid them by running away, as one can from a stimulus. The instinct is therefore identified by its:

▶ source – *excitation within the body*
▶ aim – *removal of that excitation*
▶ object – *usually external.*

Eros and Thanatos

For a long time Freud was puzzled by the tendency of patients to continually repeat and relive unpleasant experiences. He called this **repetition compulsion**. He found that it happens after a sudden and unexpected shock. Freud decided that the experience was repeated so that the normal anxiety that prepares us for danger could be built up and dealt with in retrospect. However, the repetition compulsion can sometimes totally take over. This phenomenon eventually led Freud to suggest that another instinct was at work – Thanatos, or the death instinct. The word *thanatos* is taken from the Greek word meaning 'death'.

When Thanatos is directed towards the self it produces self-destructive behaviour, such as addictions. Turned outwards it results in aggressive behaviour. The opposite of Thanatos is Eros, the life instinct (from Eros, the Greek god of love). Eros is concerned with survival of the species and is responsible for sexual and reproductive behaviour.

Freud's argument for the existence of Thanatos can be summarized as follows:

▶ *All behaviour is aimed at reducing tension and achieving a previously existing state of stability.*
▶ *Since we were all originally made from inert matter, then perhaps we are really trying constantly to return to this state.*
▶ *So the aim of all life is death, a state where there are no tensions at all because no stimuli can impinge from within or without to disturb the everlasting peace.*

This seems like a very negative way of looking at things, but this perhaps arose partly because Freud's own later life became very difficult and full of pain. He lived through the horrors of the First World War and then suffered the death of a daughter in 1920 and a grandson in 1923. His first operation for oral cancer came in 1923 – the first of 33 such operations, which must have left him in constant pain and discomfort for the rest of his life. It is to his credit that he never gave up, but kept on thinking and working until the end. However, his dualistic theory of Eros and Thanatos as two opposing forces that control all our behaviour obviously does not satisfy modern scientific thinking.

Character

The kind of family a person is born into, plus the experiences they have as they grow up, both contribute to the formation of character. According to Freud, traumatic experiences in childhood have an especially strong effect, and many of these traumas can be linked with a particular stage of development. Fixation at any of the stages will have a particular effect on the adult personality.

Fixation at the oral stage may occur if a baby is weaned too soon, or frustrated in some way when feeding. This may lead to the development of an 'oral passive' character. Such a person tends to be dependent on others, and may seek oral gratification by over-eating, drinking or smoking. The 'oral aggressive' person, on the other hand, is stuck at the teething stage, when the baby first begins to bite. This shows up later as aggressive behaviour, and the tendency to bite on objects such as pencils.

Fixation at the anal stage may give rise to an 'anal expulsive', or 'anal aggressive' character if the parents have been too obsessive about praising a child for producing wonderful bowel movements. Such a person will be very untidy and disorganized, but also generous. On the negative side, they may be aggressive and destructive, or prone to vandalizing things. Conversely, parents who are too strict about potty training and scold the child for making messes will tend to produce the opposite – an 'anal retentive' character. This type of person tends to be obsessively neat and tidy, dictatorial and mean – the classic 'control freak'.

Fixation at the phallic stage can also occur, but nobody has given a name to the type of characters that it produces. For example, some people feel a lack of self-worth sexually because they are stuck at this stage. A boy who is rejected by his mother and threatened by an over-aggressive father may react either by withdrawing into being very studious or by showing off sexually and becoming very macho. Similarly, a girl who is rejected by her father and feels threatened by trying to compete with a very feminine mother may react either by being very shy, or by becoming very feminine and seductive herself.

There are various other phallic personalities that may arise as a result of being stuck at this stage. The main point is that it is very difficult for parents to strike the correct balance: if their children are either frustrated or over-pampered in some way then they will have problems later!

THINGS TO REMEMBER

▶ *Freud established a useful new model of the ways in which we develop into adult human beings.*

▶ *He provided a map of the different levels of thinking and behaviour, which are now usually called id, ego and super-ego.*

▶ *Conflicts between the different levels result in anxiety and stress.*

▶ *Instinctive drives are held in check by a complex system of defence mechanisms. These appear in normal people as well as neurotics.*

▶ *Problems in the defence system can eventually lead to neurosis or even psychosis.*

▶ *Freud identified two opposing instincts that are often referred to as Eros and Thanatos; the life instinct and the death instinct.*

▶ *Character is modified by the experiences a child has at each stage of development.*

9

Freud and society

In this chapter you will learn:
* *Freud's theories about civilization and its effects upon the individual*
* *key aspects of his thoughts about war and religion*
* *how he applied psychoanalysis to art and literature.*

Civilization

Eventually Freud became interested in extending his psychoanalytical theories beyond individual psychology to exploring group psychology in all kinds of different areas such as anthropology, sociology, art, literature, war and religion. In 1912 he founded *Imago*, a journal of applied psychoanalysis, in order to extend his insights. He also began to invite non-medical people to join the Vienna Psychoanalytical Association in order to widen his contacts and increase the field of study for psychoanalysis. From its original beginning as a way of helping people with neurotic illnesses, psychoanalysis grew to explore child development and the structure of the psyche.

Following experiences working with traumatized soldiers after the First World War, Freud then moved on to explore the ways in which society works and the effects that it has upon the individual. He devoted most of his energy to this more sociological approach to thinking during the last two decades of his life. Four of Freud's works in particular are very important in explaining some of his thoughts about civilization and religion:

▶ *Totem and Taboo, a collection of four essays, published together in a single volume in 1913*
▶ *The Future of an Illusion, published in 1927*
▶ *Civilization and its Discontents, published in 1930*
▶ *and finally three essays, published right at the end of his life in 1939, called Moses and Monotheism.*

Freud saw civilization as representing the ways in which human life has raised itself above its primitive animal origins, but he took the view that civilization oppressed people because it imposed all kinds of rules that demanded the suppression of libidinal urges. The purpose of human life is the pursuit of happiness, dominated by the pleasure principle. By happiness, Freud means satisfaction of libidinous needs, but these are often dammed up. The ego has to find ways of controlling libidinal urges, sublimating them so that society will approve of behaviour. The need to conform in order to remain within a social group demands great sacrifices from the individual and eventually leads to a great deal of unhappiness and the formation of neurotic symptoms.

Freud sees beauty, order and cleanliness as being the features of civilized living. Justice is the first requirement in maintaining these – the law must not be broken in favour of the individual. The two main reasons for living together in societies are:

▶ *the need to get together in order to share the workload;*
▶ *to provide security within relationships, e.g. man and woman, mother and child.*

In order to gain these advantages people must curb sexual and aggressive urges, so it is difficult to live in a society and be happy. Aggressive urges are turned inwards towards the self, causing a sense of guilt and a need for punishment. This is the essence of the Oedipal complex, whereby the infantile instinctual urge to possess the mother sexually is repressed for fear of action by external authority. As the child matures, the internal sense of authority – the super-ego – gradually takes over and regulates behaviour. Freud says that the sense of guilt is the most significant problem in the development of civilization. Any thwarted instinctive urge heightens the sense of guilt and increases the problem of people trying to live happily together.

The conflicting needs of society versus the individual lead to a constant battle between ego and altruism. The essence of this battle is – 'do I answer my own needs, or do I try to fit in with other people?' Freud suggests that this battle is what causes neurosis and that it is possible that entire civilizations can develop a sort of mass neurosis and a communal super-ego. An obvious example would be the dictator leading the mass of followers. Freud's view of human nature became increasingly disillusioned and he felt that people constantly underestimated the things of true value in life, tending instead to value power, status and wealth. These words certainly have a prophetic ring to them in the modern world.

Curiously however, Freud seems to abandon his usual stance that sexual urges are the all-important driving force when he speaks about the conflict between the individual and society. He says that most people can fulfil their sexual needs within the confines of society's rules. The thing they really cannot cope with is their neighbours, because people are by nature aggressive and obnoxious towards others. However, he considered the Christian solution to this problem, crystallized in the commandments, 'thou shalt love thy neighbour as thyself' and, 'love thine enemies', to be impossible in any practical sense. Instead, he suggested that each individual try to become aware of his own repressed conflicts and cope with his own aggressive urges through a process of self-enlightenment. His hope was that eventually people would be able to abandon religion and that the intellect would reign supreme.

Religion

Freud was an atheist and basically dismissed the whole idea of there being a god, saying that this was an illusion created to protect people from their insecurity when they have outgrown their parents. He seems to base all his ideas on patriarchal, **monotheistic** religions and very much emphasizes the idea of God as a father figure. Because he sees religion as an illusion he suggests that ideally it should be abandoned. He admits, however, that this would be difficult in practice because religion forms the basis for our rules of law and order, and the human race is not sufficiently advanced yet to cope without it.

Totem and Taboo is a collection of four essays, which had originally been published separately, that looks at religious ideas within primitive societies. It is subtitled *Some points of agreement between the mental life of savages and neurotics* so, clearly, Freud was trying to draw parallels between the behaviour of primitive people and the problems encountered by his patients. Freud attempted to explore the way things had worked in primitive societies, before civilization had grown up and imposed all the suppressive influences suffered by modern humans. At the time when *Totem and Taboo* was written there was still very poor understanding of primitive, preliterate societies, so many of Freud's ideas don't have much foundation in truth, and much of his source information is now discredited. It was generally assumed that the descent of man had followed an orderly progress – from infantile 'savages' to the wonderful pinnacle of greatness that humankind occupied by the beginning of the twentieth century. Today, this vision of progress seems arrogant and in many ways misguided because we are beginning to realize that we have got a lot of things very sadly wrong and our so-called primitive ancestors have much to teach us about how to behave.

Freud said that many primitive people have special **totems**, such as animals, plants or other natural objects such as stones, which are held in symbolic reverence.

Insight

A totem is held in symbolic reverence and also watches over the tribe and helps to define certain social behaviours. Special myths are usually associated with the totem.

Groups of people share a particular totem and this tends to define their social rules, in that members of a totem group are usually forbidden from having sexual relationships. Freud noticed that many such totems took on animal forms and he assumed that these animals represented protectors. He observed two contradictory customs in association with totem animals:

▶ *the animal must not be hunted, killed or eaten, because it represents the essence of the tribal god*
▶ *but an annual feast would be held, involving rituals where the animal was killed and eaten.*

Freud suggested that modern laws forbidding murder and incest had their origin in such practices. His theory is that a primitive tribe would form a patriarchy, where one particular leader had total power to decree sexual laws and taboos. Such a society depends upon strict sexual laws to define relationships between families. These laws are the basis of culture and communication.

Insight

A taboo is a strong social prohibition against certain behaviours, words, concepts, actions, subjects of discussion and so on. Breaking a taboo is usually considered unacceptable and may even be illegal. On the other hand it can sometimes be fun and liberating!

Freud assumes that the totem represents the father of the tribe. This patriarch would expel all the younger males and keep all the females for himself. Eventually, the outcast young sons would rebel, banding together and returning to kill the patriarch in order to gain power. Their resulting guilt is expressed and expunged in the symbolic annual feast, where the totem is killed and eaten. Freud draws parallels here with the Oedipus story, saying that it is evidently universal that men desire their mothers and wish to kill their fathers. His thinking reflects the view current at the time; that primitive people are infantile in their behaviour.

Freud suggests that these ambivalent totemic religious practices are similar to the behaviour of people suffering from obsessional neurosis, which is a mental illness characterized by obsessional urges or ideas. In both cases he suggests that guilt is strongly present because a rule against incest has been broken. The obsessional neurosis is a defence against the incestuous urges of childhood, whereas the totemic feast represents the same kind of defence on a larger scale. It seems that Freud is guilty of generalizing again here – it is likely that in many cases of obsessional neurosis later events in life are the underlying cause, rather than events occurring in early childhood. For example, in a well-known case from literature, Lady Macbeth endlessly washes her hands as a symbolic way of cleansing herself of the blood of a murdered victim.

Freud also explores the idea of omnipotence of thoughts – the idea that if you think something it is more likely to happen. Freud observed this kind of omnipotence in his obsessional patients and in the fantasies of childhood. Primitive people have no problem with the idea, because to them there is no sharp division between internal and external reality. Later, however, they transfer the omnipotent power to their gods and, eventually, in the light of scientific rationality, it is abandoned altogether. Therefore, said Freud, religion is simply the tail end of a tribal neurosis.

Much of Freud's thinking in *Totem and Taboo* was based on theories such as those in Darwin's *Descent of Man*, which are now mostly discredited. For example, the totemic feast he describes is actually rare in tribes who have totems, and there is no evidence that humans ever lived in tribes dominated by a single male as do some other primates. He also overlooks the fact that some primitive people actually have matriarchal societies.

According to Freud, the Moses story has the same basic theme of breaking an incestual taboo. In *Moses and Monotheism*, Freud suggests that Moses was not actually Jewish in origin, but Egyptian. Following the revolutionary teaching of the pharaoh Akhenaten, Moses rejected the idea of a whole pantheon of gods, and began to teach his tribesmen the idea that there was only one, supreme father god. Eventually Moses led his people out of Egypt to find the Promised Land, but Freud suggests that he was subsequently murdered by some of his own tribesmen who then experienced God's wrath. They could only escape from this uncomfortable situation by promising total obedience to God from then on. The whole unfortunate episode gave rise to a lasting sense of guilt in the Jewish people, and to a longing for a messiah who could come and sort it all out. Not surprisingly, *Moses and Monotheism* is one of Freud's less popular books.

According to Freud, the principle tasks of civilization are:

▶ *to defend people against the perils of nature, such as famine, flood and disease*
▶ *to control and regulate instincts such as incest, cannibalism and lust for killing*
▶ *to demonstrate achievements that are considered worth striving for.*

He suggested that 'the gods' evolved to play a parental role, protecting people and watching over them. Their task was:

▶ *to protect people from the perils of nature*
▶ *to reconcile people to the cruelty of fate, especially death*
▶ *to compensate for the suffering imposed by civilization.*

Freud was chiefly concerned with the psychological significance of the suggested functions of religion. Religious rituals give the individual protection from the unruly libidinal urges arising from within and so enable the person to function within a group. Religion has another advantage – it promises an after life, which not only lessens the fear of death but also suggests that the person will be rewarded eventually for suppressing some of his instinctive urges. Freud does not seem to have understood the ecstatic and mystical states that many people associate with religion, and barely considers them at all. He dismisses such states, comparing them with being in love. Both states, he says, are examples of regression to a very early stage, where the individual has not learned to distinguish himself from his mother, or from the external world.

Although he had a tendency to generalize on the basis of very slim evidence, Freud claimed to be offering scientific explanations for all these ideas about religion; at the same time he was very dismissive of religious teachings because they were not scientific. He was not very interested in philosophy either, saying dismissively that it was mere playing with words. He argued that people should always try to be down-to-earth in their thinking and view the world objectively – curiously, he seems here to overlook the role of the unconscious in human thinking.

Freud always claimed to be a scientific thinker.

At the heart of Freud's criticism of religion is the fact that its teachings cannot be verified. To Freud religious ideas are illusions – fulfilments of the oldest, most primal needs. Religious questions lead people to be introspective and not scientific and this can lead towards self-deception. Freud does, rather grudgingly, admit that religious teachings have undoubtedly helped to build and maintain civilization, but says that they have also discouraged free thinking. He also admits that he too may be chasing an illusion, concluding that although science itself is not an illusion we may place too much emphasis upon its teachings.

Thoughts about war

During the First World War, Freud at first supported the Austro-German Alliance for which members of his family fought. However, he was a pacifist at heart and became very disillusioned with war.

In 1915 he wrote two short pieces describing his thoughts about war. He expressed his bewilderment as the nations of the civilized world slaughtered one another and destroyed so much that science, technology and art had strived to achieve. Freud recognized the gap between what passes as acceptable behaviour for a state and what is expected of the individual. He also saw that the state demanded complete obedience from its people, and yet treated them like children by its censorship of the truth. His sense of disillusionment increased as he observed:

▶ *the low morality shown in the behaviour of states*
▶ *the brutality that emerged in the behaviour of individuals, who used war as an excuse to unleash aggression.*

Freud said that these two observations proved that deep down human nature consists of instinctive impulses, therefore we can never totally eradicate evil. A person can be 'good' in one set of circumstances and 'bad' in another. People conform and obey because they both need love and fear punishment.

Freud is not really trying to say that it is impossible for humans to behave in a civilized fashion. He actually says that people have overestimated their own capabilities – we are not as highly evolved as we had thought we were. If we were less demanding of ourselves, this would lead to less disillusionment and the ability to be more open and honest.

The war made Freud think about people's attitude towards death. Before the war he said people had tended to pretend that death did not exist. War forced them to believe in it and took them back to a primeval state when death was a part of life's daily struggle, and man had no scruples about killing. It was Freud's work with victims of war trauma and shell shock that led him to develop his ideas about repetition compulsion (whereby the sufferer repeats often trivial actions) and Thanatos, the death instinct (see Chapter 8).

Freud lived to see the start of the Second World War as well. Hitler had come to power in Germany in 1933 and there was a public burning of Freud's books in Berlin. Freud saw this as progress, saying that it was an improvement upon what would have happened in the Middle Ages, when they would have burned him too. Little did he realize what horrors were about to be unleashed and how wrong he was about the idea of progress – fortunately Freud was spared the horror of the Holocaust, although several members of his family were victims. One wonders what he would have thought and felt about it. His fellowship with other Jews mattered to him and he had belonged to a Jewish club in Vienna, even though he did not follow the Jewish religion.

Another Jew to flee from Nazism was Albert Einstein, and a letter from him in 1932 persuaded Freud to write again about war. Freud replied that war was more a problem for statesmen to worry about, but he tried to arrive at some psychological insights:

- *Usually conflicts of interest among humans are settled by the use of violence.*
- *Several weak people can combine to overcome one strong one.*
- *A community is held together by emotional ties.*
- *Problems arise within a community when suppressed members begin to want more power.*
- *The instincts of love and hate are both essential – you cannot have one without the other.*

156

Freud therefore concluded that war could only be prevented if a central authority was set up which had the right to settle all conflicts of interest. To this end he suggested educating a special elite, with independent open minds, who would 'give direction to the dependent masses'. Ironically, this sounds curiously similar to what the Nazis had in mind. In the final paragraph of the letter, Freud speaks of himself and, by implication, Einstein, as pacifists, but he adds that there is no telling how long it will be until the rest of mankind follows suit.

Art and literature

Freud wrote about art and literature partly in order to verify his own theories about neurotic symptoms, dreams, jokes and parapraxes, and partly to try to create a theory of culture from the viewpoint of psychoanalysis. He said that writers and artists had great insight into the workings of the unconscious, which he saw underlying all cultural and psychic phenomena. He ranked the works of Homer, Sophocles, Goethe and Shakespeare as being especially great – and conveniently they fitted in well with his psychoanalytical interpretations. Because he saw the unconscious underlying all art and literature, he said that the usual psychic mechanisms were at work within them, for example repression of unacceptable urges, condensation, displacement and so on. In fact, he believed that basically all art and literature was the result of the sublimation of libidinous urges. Daydreams and fantasies were ways of evading the tedious grip of the reality principle. Artists and writers actually allowed themselves to live in their fantasy world, effectively evading the reality principle and then using their fantasies in creative ways. This cunningly avoids the worse peril of becoming a sexual pervert or neurotic, and at the same time converts the subjective repressed material into an objective, socially acceptable form. The work that is created can then have a powerful effect on others, even those who are not personally known to the artist and who are not aware of the source of their own emotion, i.e. their own repressed libidinal urges.

Freud gives an example of this phenomenon at work in the life of a creative artist in a short work called *Leonardo da Vinci and a Memory of his Childhood* (published in 1910; see Volume XI of the *Standard Edition of the Psychological Works of Sigmund Freud*). In this study, Freud uses psychoanalysis to examine Leonardo's emotional life from early childhood and, in particular, his alleged homosexuality. He argues that Leonardo's work is a prime example of libidinal urges being sublimated into creative work: in an age where art was often sensual, Leonardo's art is not expressly sexual, therefore repression is obviously at work.

Freud then goes on to look at an interesting recollection of the artist's early childhood, which is recorded in one of Leonardo's many notebooks. In this recollection, presumably a fantasy or a dream, a vulture flies down to his cradle and, opening his mouth with its tail, strikes him many times upon the lips. Freud interprets this odd vision as expressing repressed homosexuality, where the bird's tail represents the penis. The urge to take this organ into the mouth is a regression to the earliest stage of the child's existence, the oral stage, when he would have suckled his mother's breast. Freud says there is a link here with Egyptian mythology too, where vultures were supposed to be only of the female sex.

There are several flaws in Freud's argument here. The bird in Leonardo's fantasy was not actually a vulture at all, but a kite, so the tenuous link to Egyptian mythology is wrong. As far as we can tell, evidence certainly points to Leonardo having been homosexual, and this would in part account for his rather secretive nature, for one could be burned at the stake in those days if proved to be homosexual. But whether he really repressed his homosexual urges is much less clear – he surrounded himself most of his adult life with beautiful young men, in particular one called Salai, who was his special companion for many years. So although his homosexuality is probably expressed in his art – many of his figures are notably androgynous – he scarcely seems to have been sublimating his desires. Freud also suggests that there is conflict between Leonardo's artistic and scientific streaks. Again there is no real evidence for this – Leonardo was a prolific and original thinker in both the analytical and creative fields and seems to have coped very happily with the two strands – indeed, they are probably the source of his genius. His renowned slowness and unreliability in completing work is seen by Freud as a symptom of inhibition, but it seems more likely, given his prodigious output, that he simply frequently got bored with a project and moved on to something else.

FREUD'S STUDY OF OTHER ARTISTS

Freud wrote various other psychoanalytical books and papers on the work of both artists and writers, the most famous of which are *Delusions and Dreams in Jensen's Gradiva*; *The Moses of Michelangelo*; and *Dostoevsky and Parricide*. The first of these, *Delusions and Dreams in Jensen's Gradiva* (published in 1907; see Volume IX of *The Standard Edition of the Complete Works of Sigmund Freud*), is one example of the way in which Freud examined the psychological motives behind the work of a writer. Jensen's *Gradiva* is a story about a young archaeologist, set in Rome and Pompeii. Given his fascination with classical history and archaeology, the setting would obviously have appealed to Freud. In the story, the hero's chance encounter with a sculpture in a museum arouses fantasies which, according to Freud, represent repressed erotic childhood fantasies. Freud hints that this theme appears elsewhere in Jensen's work and points to an early incestuous relationship in the writer's life – another example of repressed childhood memories being channelled into artistic work.

Freud tends to liken the artist or writer to a child at play, living in an escapist world. The very young infant is governed by wish fulfilment according to the pleasure principle, which Freud says uses the variety of mental processing he called primary process. Later, when the reality principle comes into play with its secondary processing – using conscious planning and logic – part of the thought activity becomes split off. This part becomes the world of fantasy and, like the dream world, it is kept free from reality testing.

Freud argues that 'normal' people ought eventually to outgrow the need for fantasy, and that happy people never fantasize because they don't need to express unfulfilled desires. Happily, modern psychology has shown that a moderate amount of fantasy in one's life is perfectly healthy, and indeed can often be a rich source of creativity. This source of original thinking is not only seen in artists and writers, but also in scientists such as Einstein.

Freud seems to have overlooked the fact that plenty of artists and writers *are* neurotic. Taking his theory to its logical limit, if everyone's libido were fully satisfied then there would be no art or literature – a depressing thought. It seems a curiously narrow-minded theory from someone who was clearly passionately interested in both art and literature.

Insight

The problem is it all depends upon what you define as neurotic, and what you define as fantasy for that matter, since we each construct our own unique version of reality.

Freud's work on the unconscious and the use of free-association techniques have had an enormous effect upon both art and literature. Artists in the twentieth century began to experiment a lot more with imagery from dreams, visions and the unconscious. This supposedly new way of thinking led to artistic movements such as surrealism.

Insight

Surrealism is a twentieth-century cultural movement which emphasizes unconscious and dream imagery in both art and literature. Surrealist art often contains weird images and strange juxtapositions, just as one might see in a dream.

However, the idea was not actually new – as long ago as the fifteenth century, Hieronymus Bosch was using grotesque and fantastic imagery in his work – but Freud's ideas led to a great fresh upsurge in interest. Biographers began to examine intimate sexual details and childhood experiences of their subjects, and novelists began to use new techniques such as the 'stream of consciousness'. This method, used for example by Virginia Woolf (1882–1941), gives the reader a detailed account of everything the character is thinking from moment to moment. It has obvious connections with the free-association technique.

THINGS TO REMEMBER

▶ *Freud eventually tried to extend his ideas about psychoanalysis from the individual to include all of human culture and society.*

▶ *He saw the purpose of human life as being the pursuit of happiness, dominated by the pleasure principle.*

▶ *Freud said that:*
  ▷ *Although civilization is necessary for our growth and safety, the pressure on the individual to conform makes it difficult for people to live happily together. Each individual ego has to find ways of controlling libidinal urges and channeling them into safe and acceptable outlets that society will approve of.*
  ▷ *Religion is an illusion, created in order to make it easier for people to cope with life and with being members of an ordered society.*
  ▷ *War gives us a glimpse of our deep animal nature and demonstrates the working of the Death Instinct.*
  ▷ *Artists and writers have great insight into the workings of the unconscious. But he saw them as escapists, who avoid the real world by living out their fantasies through their work.*

▶ *Despite this last, somewhat cynical view, Freud's work on dreams and the unconscious has greatly influenced artists and writers in the twentieth century.*

10

Psychoanalysis

In this chapter you will learn:
- *some basic techniques of psychoanalysis*
- *details about some of Freud's own cases*
- *how psychoanalysis grew and gave rise to many modern forms of therapy.*

The process of psychoanalysis

Modern psychoanalysts do not usually completely adhere to Freud's recommendations about how to conduct therapy sessions. Nevertheless, the basic techniques used today by analysts and other psychotherapists are still similar to those used by Freud. As described earlier in this book, Freud emphasized three aspects of the therapy process that are particularly important:

▶ *the free-association technique (see Chapter 3)*
▶ *transference and counter-transference (see Chapter 3)*
▶ *the analysis of dreams (see Chapter 4).*

Freud had some strict ground rules regarding who would make a suitable patient for psychoanalysis. He insisted that the people he took on were reasonably well educated and of fairly reliable character. Psychotic patients and others with more severe types of mental disorders were not suitable. Nor were people over the age of 50, partly, he said, because the sheer volume of material that they would have to wade through was too great and the treatment would have to be prolonged. He also claimed that older people were too set in their ways to benefit from psychoanalysis. Nowadays, however, analysts often take on older patients and treat them successfully.

Freud suggested a trial period of analysis over a week or two before a full commitment was made. This was mainly because more severe mental disturbances may not be immediately apparent. His usual method, once the analysis was in progress, was to try and see a person every day, apart from weekends and holidays, because he maintained that breaks in the process were often detrimental to progress. Nowadays this is not usually a feasible way to do things, and not many people would be able to afford the fees incurred.

Freud always tried to maintain the scientific approach and remain as detached as possible. He tended to sit behind his patient, who would be lying comfortably on a couch. This was partly because he found it too wearing if he was face to face with people all day, and also because he thought it better if the patient did not see the analyst's changes of expression. He warned against becoming too familiar, suggesting that the analyst should try to be like a surgeon with his patient, putting aside his own feelings and focusing on the operation in hand. Nowadays many analysts adopt a more relaxed attitude and sit facing their patients. However, most analysts do try to guard against becoming too emotionally involved, or revealing much of their own personal life to the patient, because this can easily take the analysis off track.

Insight

Carl Jung was one of the first analysts to sit facing his patient. This helped people to see him as a human being, rather than just as a doctor.

Freud also warned that it was not a good idea to attempt an analysis of anybody who is personally known to the analyst, saying that this may lead to the break-up of friendships. He broke this rule himself, however, when he analysed his daughter Anna. He also sometimes chatted about his family to patients and was not really as stern and detached as his popular image tends to suggest.

Some of Freud's own cases

Freud's own case histories make very interesting reading and, like most of his work, they are written in a way that is easy to follow. Altogether he mentions 133 cases briefly, but there are only six that are discussed at length. One of these – Judge Schreber – was never actually seen by Freud. We have already discussed one of the others in Chapter 3 – the analysis of Dora, whose real name was Ida Bauer. Another was an unnamed lesbian of 18, whose treatment did not continue for very long. The remaining three are worth looking at in more detail.

LITTLE HANS

Little Hans (real name Herbert Graf, 1903–73) was a five-year-old boy who had a terrible phobia of horses. He was afraid to go out into the street for fear of seeing them and he also dreaded seeing heavily loaded vehicles, which he feared would topple over. Freud only saw the boy once in his consulting rooms – the rest of the time he gleaned information about dreams, conversations and behaviour from the child's father and made suggestions as to what might help. It is interesting that the father was a colleague of Freud's, which meant that he was again breaking one of his own rules about who should be taken on for analysis.

Freud saw the case as a study of castration anxiety, resulting from several factors including the birth of a younger sister, an emerging Oedipus complex, and anxiety about masturbation. During the course of the analysis Hans' behaviour did in fact improve, possibly because he was getting more attention from his father. Whatever the truth of the matter, Freud reported meeting Hans later as a strapping lad of 19 who suffered from no troubles or inhibitions.

> Freud's explanation of Little Hans' problem is an example
> of how he would sometimes jump to conclusions in order to
> fit his theories. It seems more likely that the child was simply
> afraid of horses – after all they can seem pretty huge and
> threatening when one is very small. The case also illustrates
> one of the problems with trying to assess the effectiveness of
> psychoanalysis: would Hans simply have got over his phobia
> anyway?

RAT MAN

This case study was published in 1909, entitled 'Some Remarks on
a Case of Obsessive-Compulsive Neurosis'. The patient, whose real
name was Ernst Lanzer (1878–1914), was a 29-year-old lawyer
who first came to see Freud in 1907. He had obsessional thoughts
and displayed obsessive behaviour. He gained his nickname from
his idea that someone who was dear to him, such as his father, or a
woman he admired, might be punished by having their body eaten
away by rats. Oddly enough, this obsession continued in relation
to the man's father even though he had died some years previously.
But the Rat Man's worst fear had originated from a story he
had been told while serving in the army. It was about an Eastern
punishment where the victim had a pot containing a rat tied to his
buttocks, with the evil intent that the rat would eventually gnaw its
way out via the person's anus.

Freud's interpretation of this obsession was that Rat Man had
conflicting urges of both love and aggression towards people who
were close to him, originating in childhood sexual conflicts. The
obsession was actually useful to the patient because it prevented
him from making difficult decisions in his current life and at the
same time warded off the anxiety that would arise if he faced his
real conflicts.

This was to be one of Freud's most successful analyses, and after
a year's treatment he was able to report that the patient had been
cured of his symptoms. Unfortunately, a long-term follow up was

not possible in this case, because the patient was killed in the First World War. Usually people who have suffered from obsessional thoughts and rituals of this type from early childhood tend to relapse, especially at times of stress. The next case is particularly interesting because it provides not only a long-term follow up, but also autobiographical material supplied by the patient himself.

WOLF MAN

The Wolf Man was a Russian, whose real name was Sergius Pankejeff, who lived from 1887–1979. The book about his case history, *The Wolf Man*, is well worth reading because it contains his own memoirs, Freud's analysis, a later analysis by Ruth Mack Brunswick, and a follow-up section by Muriel Gardiner, who knew the Wolf Man personally. This makes the book quite unique and provides us with not only a fascinating psychoanalytical case history, but also an intimate human story and many interesting glimpses of history.

The Wolf Man suffered from long bouts of severe depression as well as from obsessional thoughts, especially about his health. Freud's account of the analysis is long and complex, but it mainly revolves around a dream the Wolf Man recalled from when he was about four years old. In this dream he saw six or seven white wolves sitting in a big walnut tree outside his bedroom window. He awoke in terror of being eaten by them. It is this dream, plus his childhood phobia of wolves, that earned him his nickname.

By a very convoluted process of analysis Freud linked the content of the wolf dream to a hypothetical scene that the Wolf Man had witnessed from his cot when he was about 18 months old. What he supposedly saw was three incidents of his parents having intercourse, with his father penetrating his mother from the rear. Having supposedly unearthed this scene from the Wolf Man's unconscious, Freud then proceeded to explain, also at great length, that the child never actually witnessed the scene at all – the whole thing was a later fantasy!

The sex scene with his parents was never actually consciously recalled by the Wolf Man, and indeed in his old age he described Freud's interpretation of his childhood wolf dream as being very far-fetched. It seems far more likely that his childhood fear of wolves stemmed partly from having lived in Russia as a small child, where wolves in the forest were a living reality, and also from having been read Grimm's fairy tales at an impressionable age.

Freud's whole analysis seems very contrived, but the gist of his conclusions probably has some element of truth in it. He suggests that repressed sexual urges, some connected with an early attempt at seduction by his sister, who was two years older, apparently wrecked Wolf Man's future sex life completely and was a major cause of his later neurosis.

However, reading the Wolf Man's own story plus those of the other contributors to the book, it seems likely that the picture was actually a very complicated one and that other factors were also at work. Mental illness was not unusual in the Wolf Man's family. His father suffered from melancholia and his mother also showed signs of neurosis, with long-term hypochondria and other obsessive behaviour. An uncle he was especially fond of developed paranoia in adulthood and spent some time in an institution. And his sister, who had a massive influence on him throughout his childhood, took her own life by poisoning herself when he was in his late teens. The Wolf Man had difficult relationships with women throughout his life, including his wife, who eventually followed in his sister's footsteps by committing suicide.

Although his family was extremely wealthy, the Wolf Man was always very neurotic about money, showing great possessiveness and unnecessary extravagance. He had inherited a huge fortune – his father had owned vast estates in Russia – but the Russian revolution and the Bolshevist regime put an end to all that and eventually he lost not only all his wealth, but all his property as well. He was forced to flee to Vienna and find himself a job. This must have been a very difficult change in circumstances for someone who had taken his wealth and rank utterly for granted in his youth. Some years after his initial analysis, the Wolf Man returned to Freud for further treatment, and this time Freud treated him for free and continued to help him out financially for some years.

Although the Wolf Man undoubtedly felt benefit from his sessions with Freud, it seems likely that this was mainly because he thought very highly of him, seeing him as a trusted friend and protective father figure in whom he could confide. He was never cured of his neurotic symptoms, and carried on having analysis in later life, first of all with Dr Ruth Mack Brunswick, and later with various other analysts. Clearly he needed all the support and attention and probably could never have functioned normally within society without it.

Early beginnings of the psychoanalytic movement

In 1902 Freud was appointed as a professor at the University of Vienna. This was mainly because of his work in the field of neurology. People in the medical and academic world were still reacting with hostility and suspicion to his controversial ideas about psychoanalysis. Freud carried on with these ideas more or less alone, but gradually a small band of followers began to gather around him. He began a little group of like-minded people called the Wednesday Psychological Society, who would meet in his waiting room. This small group included William Stekel (a writer and psychotherapist) and Alfred Adler (an Austrian ophthalmologist and psychiatrist). Each week one of the members would give a talk about new ideas, followed by refreshments and then a discussion.

The group soon expanded by word of mouth, and by 1906 there were 17 members. Eventually the group evolved into the Vienna Psychoanalytic Society. Otto Rank (an Austrian, non-medical analyst, who was the first and most valued of Freud's pupils) was appointed as secretary and he kept minutes of the meetings and the accounts. By 1907 the group was getting more cosmopolitan – a Russian called Max Eitingon joined them, followed by some Swiss recruits from the Burghölzli Mental Hospital in Zurich, Ludwig Binswanger, Carl Jung and Karl Abraham. Freud and Jung got on especially well and a kind of father–son relationship developed between them, Freud being nearly 20 years older than Jung. Freud was particularly pleased that Jung was a gentile, because this rescued the psychoanalytic movement from accusations that it was an all-Jewish organization.

Over the next year the Hungarian doctor Sándor Ferenczi joined the group, then Ernest Jones, who was a young Welsh neurologist, and Abraham Brill from America. Eitingon and Karl Abraham went on to establish psychoanalysis in Berlin and Ferenczi did the same in Budapest. Jones and Brill were the first to introduce psychoanalytic thinking into the English language. In 1908 Jones went to Toronto, Canada, and from there he worked to spread Freud's ideas in Canada and the USA. In 1913 he founded the London Psychoanalytical Society, which had expanded enough by 1919 to be renamed the British Analytical Society. Meanwhile, Freud was gaining respect and fame elsewhere in Europe too, and the first International Congress of Freudian Psychology took place in Salzburg in 1908.

By 1909 Freud was well known internationally and he went with Jung and Ferenczi to America to lecture. The first *International Journal of Psychoanalysis* was published the same year, and Freud was awarded an honorary degree from Clark University, Massachusetts. The next year the International Psychoanalytic Association was formed. International progress was fairly slow until the end of the First World War. In 1920 the Institute of Psychoanalysis was opened in Berlin, followed by further institutes in London, Vienna and Budapest. Courses were held for students and free treatment was offered for people who could not afford the fees. Institutes were opened in the USA in New York (1931) and Chicago (1932).

Rifts in the psychoanalytic movement

Right from the start, there tended to be arguments and disagreements within the psychoanalytic movement. People were keen to develop their own theories and some accused others of inventing case histories to fit their theories. Arguments arose about the way the society was organized, and about psychoanalytic methods and issues such as the unconscious. To make matters worse, the group was constantly under outside attack from the scientific establishment and the press.

All these undercurrents led to various breaks and upheavals, and some of Freud's supporters eventually set up their own schools. Meanwhile, beginning in 1912, a secret committee, initiated by Ernest Jones, rallied round to support Freud. This loyal group originally consisted of Jones, Ferenczi, Rank, Sachs and Karl Abraham. Later, in 1919, Eitingon joined as well, as did Freud's daughter Anna. But despite the influence of this inner circle, the group gradually lost further members and it finally dissolved 20 years after it had first begun.

ALFRED ADLER

Adler was a Viennese Jew, one of the first members of the Wednesday group. He did not agree with the idea of repressed sexual impulses being the cause of neurosis. He maintained that the urges that caused all the trouble were aggressive, not sexual. Adler believed that a person's biological make-up was the most important thing – if a person had a particular handicap then they would work all the harder in order to overcome feelings of inferiority.

Adler had been President of the Vienna Society, but he resigned in 1911. He was followed in 1912 by Stekel, who refused to believe in the overwhelming importance of the unconscious. Adler began his own group, which was eventually to be called the Society for Individual Psychology.

OTTO RANK

Rank had been a protégé of Freud, who had encouraged and supported his education. For a long time he was loyal to Freud, but eventually he moved away from the group. His main complaint was that he felt the period of analysis was too long and he suggested that it should be shortened. He also saw childhood traumas, especially the Oedipus complex, as being less important than Freud considered them to be. For Rank it was the trauma of birth itself that mattered. He worked for eight years in Paris and then eventually moved to America in 1934 to continue his career there.

CARL JUNG

Jung was Freud's favourite for some years. Freud treated him like a son and wanted him to be his successor. In 1910 he was appointed as the President of the newly formed International Psychoanalytic Society. However, there had already been suggestions of problems in his relationship with Freud before then.

The year before, while they were waiting to board a ship to go to America, tension was in the air. Freud had found out that Jung had been having an illicit affair with one of his patients; Jung retaliated by being rather hostile towards Freud. He irritated him by going on and on about some mummified peat bog men that were being dug up in northern Germany. This was possibly done deliberately as a dig at Freud, teasing him about what he saw as 'mummified' or antiquated views. Freud got very agitated and eventually fainted. Later he said that this was because Jung had a death wish against him.

Worse was to come as Jung began to develop new theories of his own. He had had reservations from the beginning, feeling that Freud tended to put him on a pedestal. His own feelings were very intense too – he said that it was almost as if he had a teenage crush on Freud. Freud had also recognized that this intensity of feeling might end up in some sort of teenage rebellion.

In 1912, Jung gave a series of lectures and seminars at Fordham University in New York. It was at this point that Jung really broke away from Freud, criticizing many of the basic theories of psychoanalysis by saying that:

▶ *The Oedipus complex was not of central importance, although Jung acknowledged its existence and coined the term Electra complex for its equivalent in women.*
▶ *Libido should not be regarded as merely sexual – Jung regarded it more as a universal life force.*
▶ *Freud's ideas about infant sexuality were wrong – Jung proposed that sexuality developed more gradually.*
▶ *Pleasure could come from all sorts of non-sexual sources. For example, a baby gains pleasure from sucking because it is fulfilling a nutritional need.*
▶ *Adult neuroses were rooted in current problems that sometimes resurrected old conflicts. These were not necessarily infantile conflicts, nor were they always sexual.*

Not long after this attack on the core concepts of psychoanalysis, Freud talked to Jung at length at a conference in Munich and felt that he had won him back into the fold. Freud then proceeded to faint again at lunch, and Jung had to carry him through into another room. Clearly Freud was deeply upset about the whole affair.

The next year, Jung lectured in London and talked once again about wanting to move psychoanalysis away from its narrow emphasis on sex. He coined the phrase **'analytical psychology'**, to describe the ideas that he was evolving. After this, letters between Freud and Jung became increasingly bitter – Jung accused Freud of behaving like a controlling father, intolerant towards new ideas. Sadly, in 1913 their friendship ceased altogether and the two men became openly hostile to one another. Before long Jung resigned his presidency of the International Psychoanalytical Association.

Shortly before the friendship broke up, Freud spoke to Jung and urged him never to abandon the sexual theory, saying rather obscurely that it was a bulwark against the occult. Jung was very taken aback, because what Freud seemed to mean by the 'occult' included the very things which most interested him – almost everything that philosophy and religion had learned about the psyche, including the newly expanding science of parapsychology. Jung made a counterattack, saying that the sexual theory itself was just as 'occult', in the sense that it was actually just the same sort of unproven hypothesis as many other speculative views.

> ## Insight
> Jung went on to develop his own school of thinking, which he called analytical psychology, partly in order to distinguish it from Freud's psychoanalysis. You can find out more about his fascinating ideas in *Jung – The Key Ideas*, by the same author.

WILHELM REICH

Reich was another member of the orthodox psychoanalytic movement who broke away much later, in 1933. He was interested in the way individuals interacted with society, and believed that a person's character was formed in this way. For him, the sexual revolution was connected with the social revolution. He was greatly influenced by Marxist thinking and worked with the communist party, thus combining psychoanalysis with politics. Because of his revolutionary ideas he had to flee from the rise of Nazism and settled in Maine in the USA. Here, in 1942, he founded the Orgone Institute, which was based on theories about the power of orgasm.

SÁNDOR FERENCZI

Even the loyal Ferenczi, who was close to Freud for many years, eventually fell into disgrace. He was a highly sensitive man, who took on many difficult cases. In collaboration with Rank and later others, he developed a form of psychoanalysis known as the 'active' technique. Unlike the remote and clinical approach advocated by Freud, this could involve open demonstrations of affection between analyst and client, even at times evolving into a kind of reciprocal analysis where client and analyst exchanged roles.

Most of the people who broke away from Freud did so because they felt that he laid too much emphasis on sex. Psychoanalysis was very difficult to understand and people were constantly coming up with new variations of their own. Freud tended to present a rather authoritarian figure, always trying to keep control and resenting the intrusion of new ideas from others. It is amusing to think of him as a sort of struggling super-ego of the psychoanalytic movement, desperately trying to control all the other egos!

Some famous followers of Freud

ANNA FREUD

Anna was Freud's youngest daughter and she nursed him through his last illness. She was a pupil of his and eventually became a psychoanalyst in her own right, and an important member of the International Psychoanalytical Association. She concentrated mainly on the ego and the various ways in which it defended itself, because she believed that there had previously been too much emphasis on the id. She was very much a supporter of her father's original ideas, but she extended them.

Anna believed that it was very important to look at defence mechanisms because they help us to understand the problems with which the ego is grappling. She tried to identify the main dangers to the ego, which she decided were:

- *instinctive urges from the id*
- *nagging from the super-ego*
- *external dangers*
- *conflict within the ego, caused by opposing tendencies, such as activity and passivity.*

Anna fled from the Nazis with her family before the war and eventually co-founded the Hampstead Child Therapy Clinic. Anna's ideas are important mainly because she derived them from direct observation of young children, rather than by talking to adults about their childhood. She was a pioneer in working with psychologically disturbed children.

Critics of Anna Freud say that she was always in her father's shadow, but this is unfair. She not only nursed her father when he was ill and saw to it that his affairs were kept in order, but she also did a great deal of the work involved in getting the family out of Vienna before the war. She published several books of her own and her career continued to flourish after Freud's death. She was, however, very loyal all her life to her father and his ideas. When she became a member of the Secret Committee she was given a ring as a token of trust and fellowship. After Freud died she had one of these rings made into a brooch which shows a picture of the Roman god Jupiter sitting on a throne, with the goddess Minerva in attendance. She died in 1982, and in 1986 the family house that had continued to be her home for 40-odd years was made into the Freud Museum, according to her wish.

MELANIE KLEIN

Melanie Klein was born in Vienna and underwent analysis with Sándor Ferenczi, before working in his children's clinic. She moved to London in 1926 and became a British citizen. She worked with disturbed adults but, like Anna Freud, her main contribution came from her work with children. Melanie Klein believed that emotions were present in children from a very young age. She observed children's emotions by watching them at play, even before they could express themselves verbally. This new way of working with children led to her being able to analyse them at a much earlier age than had previously been thought possible, even as young as two years old.

Although Klein was seen by some as Freud's successor, she opposed his thinking in various ways. Eventually she formed her own group of analysts, the Kleinians, within the British Psychological Society, because her ideas had diverged so much from Freud's original ideas. She believed that the forerunner of the super-ego began to form much earlier than Freud had stated, during the first two years of life. For her the aggressive drive was the important one, rather than the sexual drive. Her arguments caused disagreements in mainstream psychoanalysis with some people, such as Anna Freud. She was one of the leading lights in the Object Relations School. This school of thought disagreed with Freud's stages of child development. It said that right from birth the mental life of a child is orientated towards an object, which can be anything in the external world – a person or a thing. The child constructs its inner world from ideas about these external objects. Conflicts arise as a result of the way in which this internalization process progresses.

Melanie Klein developed the technique of play therapy, which is now used to help children worldwide. Instead of using free association, which is impossible with very young children, she encouraged them to express their feelings through play and drawing. In this way analysts can grasp something of what is going on in the child's unconscious mind through non-verbal behaviour.

KAREN HORNEY

Karen Horney was an analyst in Berlin during the 1920s and 1930s and then joined the staff at the New York Psychoanalytical Institute. She was particularly interested in social factors in psychological development and eventually her ideas evolved away from the mainstream. Many people in the psychoanalytical movement have taken a rather closed-shop attitude, saying that people who are not analysts will never be able fully to understand psychoanalytical theory. Like Adler, Karen Horney wrote for the general reader and her ideas became very popular in America. She even wrote one of the first self-help books and developed the idea of self-analysis, suggesting that for more minor problems people could become their own analyst. This idea has unsurprisingly not gained much support from other analysts, but there is now a huge range of self-help and personal development books on the market.

Karen Horney maintained that social influences are much more important than underlying fixed biological patterns in developing neuroses. She said that the latter idea was too deterministic and out of date. She argued against the idea of an Oedipus complex, saying that there was no such thing as a universal child psychology. She maintained that the worst thing that could happen to a child – the 'basic evil'- was to encounter a total lack of warmth and love. She pointed out that many children survive incidents of incest and aggression so long as they have someone who loves and appreciates them.

Karen Horney was also interested in women's psychology. She said that women's feelings of inferiority were caused by oppression from society, rather than by a biologically determined castration complex. She also challenged Freud's theory of penis envy in women, saying that although a few women may suffer from it, it is by no means universal. In fact, she suggested that there was a male version, 'womb envy', because some men are jealous of women's ability to bear children.

ERICH FROMM

Fromm was born in Germany and trained as a social psychologist and psychoanalyst. Later he worked with Karen Horney and H. S. Sullivan. He was interested in the individual's relationship with society. He said that different cultures produce different psychological types, and the work of anthropologists has tended to show that he was right. The Oedipus complex has indeed turned out not to be universal – there are big differences in child-rearing habits, family structure, social rules and so on.

Fromm's ideas differed from those of Freud in two very fundamental ways:

▶ *A person's main challenge comes from the way he relates to others in society and not from the struggle with instinctive urges.*
▶ *Relationships between man and society are constantly changing. Freud had taken the view that the relationship was*

static – mankind was basically evil and society's job was to tame him.

Fromm suggested that there were various basic human needs which went far beyond the purely biological needs that Freud claimed to rule all our behaviour. If these needs were not met, then mental health problems could arise:

▶ Relatedness – *we all need other human beings to relate to in our lives – in other words we all need love. If this need is not met, a person may try to find love in other ways, for example by submitting to somebody harsh and domineering, as in the battered wife scenario, or by giving their life over totally to religion.*
▶ Creativity – *the urge to be creative may appear in all kinds of ways, such as having children, writing books, painting or gardening. If this need is not met, people may become destructive instead, for example, they might start vandalizing telephone boxes, which gives them a feeling of power.*
▶ Rootedness – *everybody needs to have roots, a sense of belonging somewhere. As we grow up and leave our mothers we need to find a different sense of belonging. Negative aspects of this need could lead to religious fanaticism, or agoraphobia, where a person feels safe only in their own tiny world.*
▶ Sense of identity – *as well as belonging to a group, we need a sense of individuality. Sometimes people will do crazy things in order to get noticed, or they may cling to a group and try taking their identity from belonging to it.*
▶ A frame of orientation – *this is about understanding the world around us, and our own place in it. Society helps us with this through education and social conditioning.*

HARRY STACK SULLIVAN

H. S. Sullivan believed that the personality was influenced by society. This is called the 'culturalist view'. Sullivan said that a person felt happy and 'good' if their behaviour fitted in with societal norms. If the reverse was true then the person felt 'bad' and insecure. This interactive view meant that it was no good trying to treat a mentally ill person in isolation, away from society. He saw the personality not as a unique, isolated thing, but more as an interaction between people. There is probably a lot of truth in this because we all see each other differently and react to one another in different ways.

Sullivan said that the early relationship between parent and child was not primarily about sex, as Freud had suggested, but about the quest for security. This was certainly true for Sullivan himself, who was starved of affection as a child and had few playmates – an interesting contrast to Freud's own start in life.

Insight

You might also like to read about the work of Jacques Lacan (1901–1981), who was a prominent French analyst.

Psychoanalysis today

Many modern therapies have their roots in psychoanalytic thinking, but these are now so many and so diverse that it is not really possible to identify one single therapy that can be called psychoanalysis. Because of this difficulty people have recently tried to define what constitutes psychoanalysis, as distinct from the innumerable other therapies. Some of the main distinguishing features are:

▶ *It is a general theory of psychology that applies to both 'normal' people and neurotics.*
▶ *Psychoanalysts follow Freud's idea that people have a mental apparatus that reacts to stimuli from both the external world and the world within.*
▶ *Psychoanalysis is concerned with the ways in which people adapt by coping with these various stimuli, and the conflicts that arise as a result.*
▶ *Mental events are seen as being subject to the law of cause and effect, according to Freud's determinist view.*

▶ *Psychoanalysis assumes the existence of the unconscious,*
   so that there are some aspects of mental life that are not
   accessible to the conscious mind.

Insight

There are many different forms of psychotherapy around
today which have their roots in Freud's talking-cure
approach. Three of the major schools are:

▶ *psychodynamic psychotherapy, which concentrates on*
   exploring childhood emotional issues and emphasizes the
   relationship between client and therapist.
▶ *cognitive behavioural therapy, which is more short-term and*
   goal-orientated, concentrating on replacing dysfunctional
   beliefs and behaviours with more helpful ones.
▶ *humanistic therapy, which focuses on the individual person,*
   and their personal development, rather than on particular
   analytical techniques.

The question of whether or not psychoanalysis is actually
effective as a treatment for neurotic disorders is not easy to
answer. It is hard to say what constitutes a 'cure'. Many people
still have neurotic symptoms and behavioural problems after many
years of analysis, so why do they continue to go and see their
analyst, and spend a lot of money on treatment? The answer is
probably quite straightforward: as in the case of the Wolf Man,
many people find their sessions helpful because they at last find
someone they can trust who will sit and listen to their problems
without being shocked and judgemental. In this way they often find
that although they still have psychological problems, they are able
to cope with them more effectively, and often form much better
relationships with other people as well.

In the early days of psychoanalysis people expected to see radical
changes in the whole personality – there was general debate about
whether or not someone had been 'completely analysed'. Nowadays
it is recognized that this is an unrealistic expectation. However,
it is almost certainly true to say that people who visit psychoanalysts,
rather than suffering in silence and hoping the problem will go

away, are often much more likely to recover from their difficulties. What psychoanalysis can do is help people to accept themselves and cope with their problems rather than becoming overwhelmed by them. The Wolf Man himself commented that if you looked at psychoanalysis critically it is all pretty unrealistic – nevertheless, he maintained that it had helped him immeasurably in coping with life and he regarded Freud as a genius.

Freud's prolific output of writing and the way he constantly changed his mind about what he thought in his relentless search for truth show us that he was very much an ideas man. He was, on the whole, more interested in the theories that lay behind psychoanalysis, rather than in their application. And, as we have seen throughout this book, he was always anxious to be seen as a detached, analytical observer – a true scientist. Nowadays, psychotherapy has moved more towards studying the importance of relationships in an individual's life from an early age, particularly emphasizing the relationship with the mother – as Freud never did.

Psychoanalysts still believe, as Freud did, that good sexual relationships are essential to health and happiness, but they believe that the ability to achieve good relationships in adulthood depends very much on the ability of the child to relate to parents, or other caretakers, in early life. This means that modern analysts are particularly concerned with looking at transference during the course of analysis, because this is a way of uncovering the dynamics of a person's early relationships. Freud, on the other hand, was rather reluctant to look too deeply into transference, because this would tend to undermine his status as a detached observer. There is some evidence, however, that later on in life he did begin to admit that he often became emotionally important to his patients.

Freud's patients tended to come to him with specific hysterical or obsessional symptoms. The modern patient is more likely to come with more general problems, to do with relationships or generally coping with life. This has led to further debate – is psychoanalysis just about removing tiresome neurotic symptoms, or is it really more about developing self-awareness? Many analysts since Freud have taken the latter view, in particular Jung, who developed his own 'analytical psychology'.

Many people have criticized Freud, saying among other things that:

▶ *he places far too much emphasis upon sex*
▶ *he claims to be scientific and yet his findings are often vague, inaccurate and based upon small samples of data*
▶ *many of his ideas were not actually original*
▶ *psychoanalysis doesn't work – in fact, it may even make people worse*
▶ *the movement has tended to have a very closed-shop attitude, claiming that you cannot grasp the theories properly unless you are an analyst yourself*
▶ *the theories are annoyingly self-fulfilling – any attack on them can be argued to be proof that they are true because it just shows that the attacker is suffering from repression.*

Peter Fonagy, Professor of Psychoanalysis at University College London, has created a new department that aims to address this type of criticism. Proper scientific research is being carried out in order to test psychological therapies in a way that Freud never did. The results so far have been interesting and are tending to challenge some of the other more modern therapies. For example, they showed that if unpublished results from drug company research were taken into consideration, the risks of giving anti-depressants to teenagers usually outweighed the advantages. Another study showed that when the part of the brain responsible for our instinctive drives is damaged, dreaming stops. This might give weight to Freud's theory that dreams express our deep, instinctive needs.

Whatever criticism it may receive, it seems that psychoanalysis in one form or another is here to stay. It is more popular than ever, especially in America. There are many books on the subject and the ideas involved are now much more accessible to the general public than they were previously. Some of the theories have been so completely absorbed into everyday thinking that its very language has become subtly incorporated into ordinary speech – we all use phrases such as 'Freudian slip', 'death wish' and 'anally retentive'.

Freud would no doubt have been gratified by the continuing wide interest and debate that have stemmed from his revolutionary ideas. Without Freud, perhaps we would not yet have begun to understand such things as:

▶ *the importance of childhood experiences in the development of the adult personality*
▶ *the existence of the unconscious and its huge influence over human behaviour*
▶ *the way we all use defence mechanisms to protect our egos*
▶ *the importance of dreams in understanding our true thoughts and feelings*
▶ *the fact that talking about a problem often leads to helping to resolve it.*

The last years of Freud's life must have been difficult to endure. He had undergone 33 operations since the initial discovery of a malignant growth on his jaw and palate in 1923. When he was old and infirm, he had to flee his homeland for a foreign country. He finally died of cancer on 23 September 1939. His ashes were laid to rest at the crematorium at Golders Green in London, in one of his favourite Greek urns. A fitting end for a great thinker.

THINGS TO REMEMBER

▶ *Freud emphasized three aspects of the therapy process:*
   ▷ *the free-association technique*
   ▷ *transference and counter-transference*
   ▷ *the analysis of dreams.*

▶ *Little Hans, Rat Man and Wolf Man are some of Freud's most famous case histories.*

▶ *The psychoanalytical movement grew slowly from humble beginnings in Vienna to become a movement of international importance.*

▶ *Right from the start there were arguments and disagreements within the group. Many people broke away, mainly because they disagreed with Freud's emphasis on the importance of the sexual.*

▶ *Carl Jung was one of those who broke away from Freud and developed his own system, called analytical psychology. (See* Jung – The Key Ideas, *by the same author.)*

▶ *Many other influential psychologists and psychiatrists have been inspired by Freud and have developed his ideas further.*

▶ *Psychoanalysis is still thriving today, although it has evolved into many different forms. Three major modern approaches are the psychodynamic, cognitive behavioural and humanistic approaches.*

▶ *Psychoanalysis undoubtedly helps many people to run their lives more effectively: this is probably mainly because an analyst has time to sit and listen in a non-judgemental way.*

Glossary

abreaction The freeing of repressed emotions.

abstract Existing in thought rather than in solid matter.

affect An emotion attached to an idea.

amnesia A total or partial inability to remember.

aphasia A neurological disorder where the patient is either unable to recognize words, or unable to pronounce them.

bourgeois Middle-class, materialistic and conservative.

cathartic method A method of therapy involving the freeing of repressed emotions.

complex A related group of ideas that are usually repressed and may cause emotional problems and conflicts.

concrete Existing in a material form.

condensation Fusion of two or more ideas in a dream.

conscious mind The part of the mind that is aware of its actions and emotions.

conversion hysteria The transformation of repressions into physical symptoms.

defence mechanism An unconscious way of protecting the ego against undesirable affects.

denial Refusing to accept the reality of a situation.

determinist Someone who believes that all events follow a rigid pattern of cause and effect.

displacement The shifting of emotions attached to one idea onto a different idea.

dynamic model A simplified description of a system, emphasizing motives and drives.

dynamic psychology A method that emphasizes that there are motives and drives for behaviour.

ego The part of the psyche which reacts to external reality and which a person sees as the 'self'.

Eros The life instinct: the basic source of all drives concerned with self-preservation and enjoyment.

erotogenic zone An area of the body where certain stimuli, especially rubbing, produce feelings of pleasure.

fixation Getting stuck at a particular stage in sexual development.

free-association A process where the client is given a word and then tells the analyst all the ideas that come to mind.

free-association technique A method used in psychoanalysis where the patient is encouraged to say whatever he or she feels, without censorship.

histology The branch of anatomy dealing with the structure of tissues.

homologous Fundamentally similar in structure and development.

hypnosis A state similar to sleep or deep relaxation, where the patient is still able to respond to the therapist and is open to suggestion.

hysteria A nervous disorder with varying symptoms.

id The unconscious part of the psyche that is concerned with inherited, instinctive impulses.

introjection Absorbing into oneself the characteristics of another person.

latency period The period of development when sexual activity is dormant.

latent content The part of a dream that is not consciously remembered before analysis.

libido Sexual drive.

manifest content The part of a dream that is consciously remembered.

mechanistic view Seeing a person as a machine whose behaviour is determined by physical or chemical causes.

monotheistic Adjective describing a religion whose doctrine holds that there is only one god.

neurology The branch of biology that studies the structure and functions of the nervous system.

neuropathology The study of diseases of the nervous system.

neurosis A minor nervous or mental disorder.

Oedipus complex The desire of the child to possess sexually the parent of the opposite sex, while excluding the parent of the same sex.

organic disease Disease that relates to particular body structures or functions.

overdetermined When more than one root cause is present.

parapraxis General term for a Freudian slip, e.g. a slip of the tongue, or forgetting someone's name.

philosophy A system of learning that investigates the underlying nature and truth of knowledge and existence.

positivism A way of thinking that limits knowledge to that which is directly observable.

preconscious The region of the mind between conscious and unconscious, where material is stored away but readily accessible.

projection Attributing taboo urges or faults to someone else.

psyche The mind, soul, or spirit.

psychiatry The study and treatment of mental illnesses.

psychoanalysis A system of psychology and method of treating mental disorders, developed by Sigmund Freud.

psychology The scientific study of the mind and behaviour.

psychopathology The study of abnormal mental processes.

psychosis Severe mental disorder.

rationalization Finding an excuse for behaviour that is more acceptable to the ego than the real reason.

reaction formation Covering up an impulse by displaying the opposite behaviour.

reductionism Analysing complex things into their simple constituents.

regression Reverting back to an earlier behaviour or developmental stage.

repetition compulsion An inner drive that causes an individual to repeat actions.

repression The process of banishing unpleasant or undesirable feelings and experiences to the unconscious mind.

resistance A process that prevents unconscious ideas from being released.

sexual aim The sexual act that a person is driven towards.

sexual object A person or thing from which the sexual attraction comes.

sublimation An unconscious process by which libido is transferred to a non-sexual, socially acceptable or safe activity.

super-ego The part of the mind that acts like an 'inner parent', giving us a conscience and responding to social rules.

symbolization Using an object or idea to represent a different object or idea.

Thanatos The death instinct: the basic source of all drives concerned with destructive behaviour, either towards the self or towards others.

totem An animal, plant, or other natural object held in symbolic reverence.

transference Emotional attitudes developed by the patient towards the analyst.

unconscious Parts of the mind and personality of which a person is not aware.

vitalism Philosophical idea that assumes non-material forces are at work in biology.

Taking it further

Timeline of important events in Freud's life

1856	Born on 6 May in Freiberg, Moravia.
1860	Family moves to Vienna.
1865	Starts Leopoldstadter Gymnasium (secondary school).
1873	Enters University of Vienna to study medicine.
1876–82	Works on anatomy and physiology under Brücke at the Institute of Physiology in Vienna.
1877	First publications of scientific papers.
1881	Graduates as doctor of medicine.
1882	Engaged to Martha Bernays.
1882–5	Works at Vienna General Hospital. Publishes many scientific papers.
1884–7	Research in clinical use of cocaine.
1885	Appointed as university lecturer in neuropathology.
1885–6	Studies under Charcot.
1886	Sets up private practice in Vienna and marries Martha Bernays.
1887	First uses hypnotic suggestion. Birth of daughter Mathilde.
1887–1902	Friendship and correspondence with Fliess.
1889	Birth of son Jean-Martin.
1890	First uses cathartic method.
1891	Writes *On Aphasia*. Birth of son Olivier.
1892	Birth of son Ernst.
1893	Birth of daughter Sophie.
1893–6	Works with Josef Breuer.
1895	Publishes *Studies in Hysteria* jointly with Breuer. Birth of daughter Anna.
1896	First coins term 'psychoanalysis'. Death of father.

1897	Beginning of self-analysis, leading to ideas about infant sexuality and the Oedipus complex.
1900	Publishes *The Interpretation of Dreams*.
1901	Publishes *The Psychopathology of Everyday Life*.
1902	Starts Wednesday Psychological Society. Appointed professor at Vienna University.
1905	Publishes *Three Essays on the Theory of Sexuality* and *Jokes and Their Relation to the Unconscious*.
1906	Beginning of friendship with Jung.
1908	First International Psychoanalytical Congress in Salzburg. Case history of Little Hans.
1909	Travels to America with Jung.
1912	Publishes *Totem and Taboo*.
1914	Publishes *On Narcissism*. Jung leaves psychoanalytical movement.
1915	Delivers Introductory Lectures at University of Vienna.
1917	Publishes *Introductory Lectures on Psychoanalysis* and *Mourning and Melancholia*.
1919	Works with soldiers traumatized by war.
1920	Publishes *Beyond the Pleasure Principle*. Death of daughter Sophie.
1921	Publishes *Group Psychology* and the *Analysis of the Ego*.
1923	Publishes *The Ego and the Id*. First diagnosis of cancer. Death of grandson Heinerle.
1926	Publishes *Inhibitions, Symptoms and Anxiety*.
1927	Publishes *The Future of an Illusion*.
1930	Publishes *Civilization and its Discontents*. Awarded Goethe prize by the City of Frankfurt. Death of mother.
1932	Exchange of letters with Albert Einstein.
1933	Public burning of Freud's books by the Nazis in Berlin.
1936	80th birthday. Made a Corresponding Fellow of the Royal Society in Britain.
1938	Hitler invades Austria. Freud moves to London with his wife and daughter Anna. Publishes *Moses and Monotheism* and *An Outline of Psychoanalysis* (unfinished).
1939	Dies in London on 23 September.

Places to visit

PRIBOR, CZECH REPUBLIC

Freud's birthplace. He was born in Zamecnicka Ulice (Locksmith Lane) – very appropriate for a man who was to unlock the secrets of the unconscious. The house where he was born has a plaque commemorating his birth and a sign with a decorative key hanging from it. It is still occupied as a residence and as a business, so you cannot look round. In a nearby plaza there is a monument consisting of three stones, one with a bust of Freud.

SITE OF THE SCHLOSS BELLEVUE, NEAR VIENNA

Here there is a monument bearing a plaque that commemorates Freud's revelation about the importance of dreams in psychoanalysis.

THE SIGMUND FREUD MUSEUM, BERGGASSE 19, VIENNA

www.freud-museum.at

This was Freud's family home until 4 June 1938. He also had his consulting rooms here. The museum contains photographs, memorabilia, documents and personal items belonging to Freud. There is an exhibition of his life and work, plus archive video and audio tapes of him, his family and colleagues.

FREUD MUSEUM, 20 MARESFIELD GARDENS, LONDON

www.freud.org.uk

This was the home of Freud and his family after they escaped from the Nazis in Vienna in 1938. It remained the family home until his daughter Anna died in 1982. The centrepiece of the museum is Freud's library and study, preserved just as they were in his lifetime, including the original psychoanalytic couch. There is a huge collection of antique furniture and artefacts from ancient Egypt, Rome, Greece and the Far East.

A list of Freud's most important works

Freud was a prolific writer and wrote many essays, papers, lectures and letters as well as full-length books. This is a list of his most important works, in chronological order:

1891	*On Aphasia*
1895	(with Breuer) *Studies On Hysteria*
1900	*The Interpretation of Dreams*
1901	*The Psychopathology of Everyday Life*
1905	*Three Essays on the Theory of Sexuality*
	Jokes and Their Relation to the Unconscious
1912	*Totem and Taboo*
1914	*On Narcissism*
1917	*Introductory Lectures on Psychoanalysis*
1917	*Mourning and Melancholia*
1920	*Beyond the Pleasure Principle*
1921	*Group Psychology and the Analysis of the Ego*
1923	*The Ego and the Id*
1926	*Inhibitions, Symptoms and Anxiety*
1927	*The Future of an Illusion*
1930	*Civilization and its Discontents*
1938	*Moses and Monotheism*
	An Outline of Psychoanalysis

Further reading

There are a huge number of books available both by and about Freud. The following brief list gives a few suggestions about where to begin further reading.

BOOKS WRITTEN BY FREUD

Freud, S. *The Standard Edition of the Complete Works of Sigmund Freud* (24 Vol.), London: Hogarth Press and the Institute of Psychoanalysis (1953–74).

1 *Pre-Psychoanalytic Publications and Unpublished Drafts* (1886–99)
2 *Studies On Hysteria* (1893–5)
3 *Early Psychoanalytic Publications* (1893–9)
4 *The Interpretation of Dreams I* (1900)
5 *The Interpretation of Dreams II* (1900–01)
6 *The Psychopathology of Everyday Life* (1901)
7 *A Case of Hysteria, Three Essays on Sexuality and Other Works* (1901–5)
8 *Jokes and Their Relation to the Unconscious* (1905)
9 *Jensen's Gradiva and Other Works* (1906–8)
10 *The Cases of Little Hans and the Rat Man* (1909)
11 *Five Lectures on Psychoanalysis, Leonardo and Other Works* (1910)
12 *Case History of Schreber, Papers on Technique and Other Works* (1911–13)
13 *Totem and Taboo and Other Works* (1913–14)
14 *A History of the Psychoanalytic Movement, Papers on Metapsychology and Other Works* (1914–16)
15 *Introductory Lectures on Psychoanalysis Parts I and II* (1915–16)
16 *Introductory Lectures on Psychoanalysis Part III* (1917)
17 *An Infantile Neurosis and Other Works* (1917–19)
18 *Beyond the Pleasure Principle, Group Psychology and Other Works* (1920–22)
19 *The Ego and the Id and Other Works* (1923–5)
20 *An Autobiographical Study, Inhibitions, Symptoms and Anxiety, Lay Analysis and Other Works* (1925–6)
21 *The Future of an Illusion, Civilization and its Discontents and Other Works* (1927–31)
22 *New Introductory Lectures on Psychoanalysis and Other Works* (1932–6)

23 *Moses and Monotheism, An Outline of Psychoanalysis and Other Works* (1937–9)
24 *Index*

Separate books by Freud include the following:

Freud, S. *The Interpretation of Dreams*, Random House Publishing Inc. (1994)

Freud, S. *The Psychopathology of Everyday Life*, Penguin (1991)

Freud, S. *Introductory Lectures on Psychoanalysis*, Penguin (1973)

Freud, S. *New Introductory Lectures on Psychoanalysis*, Penguin (1973)

Freud, S. *Moses and Monotheism*, Random House (1987)

Freud, S. *Jokes and Their Relation to the Unconscious*, WW Norton & Co (1963)

Freud, S. *Three Essays on the Theory of Sexuality*, Basic Books (1988)

Freud, S. *Totem and Taboo*, WW Norton & Co (1989)

Freud, S. *Future of an Illusion*, WW Norton & Co (1989)

Freud, S. *The Penguin Freud Library* (15 Vol.), Penguin (1991) (has many of Freud's more important works in paperback)

Freud, S., Freud, A. (Ed.) *Essentials of Psychoanalysis*, Penguin (1991)

BOOKS ABOUT FREUD AND HIS WORK

Jones, E. *The Life and Work of Sigmund Freud*, Penguin (1974)

Gay, P. *Freud: A Life for Our Times*, Dent (1998)

Ferris, P. *Dr Freud: A Life*, Sinclair-Stevenson Ltd (1997)

Gay, P. *The Freud Reader*, Norton (1995)

Storr, A. *Freud*, Oxford (1989)

Wilson, S. *Sigmund Freud*, Sutton (1997)

Wollheim, R. *Freud*, Fontana (1991)

Clark, R. W. *Freud: The Man and the Cause*, Granada (1982)

A psychoanalytical case history:

The Wolf Man. *The Wolf Man*, Hill and Wang (1991)

BOOKS ABOUT PSYCHOANALYSIS

Rycroft, C. *A Critical Dictionary of Psychoanalyis*, Penguin (1972)

Malcom, J. *Psychoanalysis: The Impossible Profession*, Picador (1980)

Fine, R. *A History of Psychoanalyis*, Columbia University Press (1979)

Bateman, A. and Holmes, J. *Introduction to Psychoanalysis: Contemporary Theory and Practice*, Routledge (1995)

Laplanche, J. and Pontalis, J. B. *The Language of Psychoanalysis*, Hogarth (1985)

ANTI-FREUD BOOKS

Eysenck, H. J. *The Decline and Fall of the Freudian Empire*, Scott-Townsend (1990)

Webster, R. *Why Freud Was Wrong: Sin, Science and Psychoanalyis*, Basic Books (1995)

Useful websites

www.freudfile.org — Freud's life and work

www.psywww.com — Psychology-related information, including entire text of *The Interpretation of Dreams*

www.answers.com — Handy website with a lot of links

www.nyfreudiansociety.org — Homepage of New York Freudian Society. Site includes a digital version of abstracts from Freud's work

www.psychoanalysis.org.uk — The Institute of Psychoanalysis and British Psychoanalytical Society

www.psychoanalysis.org — New York Psychoanalytic Society and Institute

There are many other psychoanalytical societies worldwide that have websites. You can also find various complete texts by Freud, and many of his letters, including correspondence with Fliess, Martha Bernays, Abraham, Jung and Einstein.

Index

....

Credits

Notes

Notes

Notes